The BATH Cook Book

A celebration of the amazing food & drink in Bath and Wiltshire.
Featuring over 30 stunning recipes.

The Bath Cook Book

©2016 Meze Publishing. All rights reserved.

First edition printed in 2016 in the UK.

ISBN: 978-1-910863-17-6

Thank you to:
David Campbell, The Royal Crescent Hotel
Helen Rich, A Taste of Bath

Compiled by: Heather Hawkins

Written by: Kelsie Marsden

Photography by:
Paul Carroll (www.paulcarrollphoto.com)
Aaron Parsons (www.aaronparsons.co.uk)
Jed Alder (www.througheye.co.uk)

Edited by: Rachel Heward, Phil Turner

Designed by: Matt Crowder, Paul Cocker,
Marc Barker

PR: Kerre Chen

Cover art: Luke Prest (www.lukeprest.com)

Contributors: Sarah Koriba

Published by Meze Publishing Limited
Unit S8 & S9 Global Works
Penistone Road
Sheffield S6 3AE
Web: www.mezepublishing.co.uk
Tel: 0114 275 7709
Email: info@mezepublishing.co.uk

Printed by Bell & Bain Ltd, Glasgow

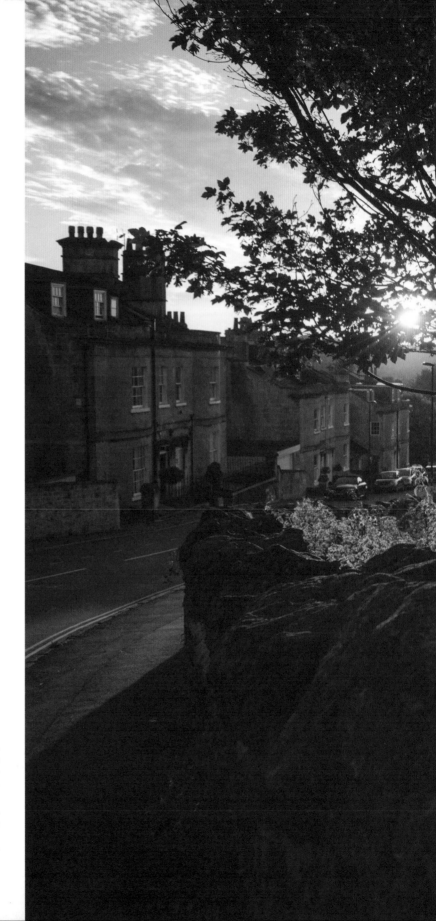

FOREWORD

Home to some of the finest afternoon teas in the country as well as a wealth of top restaurants, stylish cafés and heart-warming gastropubs, Bath is a foodie haven that oozes history from every pore.

Bath is a wonderful city and I feel very fortunate to work here, especially in such an amazing, iconic building. It's a beautiful place with a real hubbub about it; my favourite time of year is autumn, the city's two universities fill back up with students who help to give the place a real buzz. There's nowhere better in the country to just walk around, stop for a coffee and absorb the atmosphere… and there are some fantastic places out there which I try to get to when I can. We need to keep supporting the innovative independents.

We're very fortunate in terms of our suppliers around this part of the country. At The Royal Crescent Hotel & Spa, we try to keep it as local as we can; as long as the quality is up to scratch of course. Yes, you can't get the same quality ham here as you can from Spain, and our langoustines come from Scotland, but still the majority of our produce comes from closer to home.

We use the likes of Eades Greengrocer on Crescent Lane for our fruit and vegetables, some of which they grow themselves while we source our beef from Ruby and White in Bristol and the rest of our meat from Bartlett and Sons in Bath; we even get our truffles from Wiltshire if we can.

So make the most of this book and the amazing places that are featured. Cook their dishes, buy their produce and eat in their restaurants. We live in a fantastic city, so let's enjoy it.

David Campbell

Executive head chef at The Dower House Restaurant, The Royal Crescent Hotel.

CONTENTS

Welcome
TO BATH

Bath has a long established reputation for good food and is home to a wealth of top restaurants, trendy cafés, stylish bars and popular gastropubs.

Enjoy a fine dining experience at one of Bath's premier hotels; The Queensberry, The Gainsborough Bath Spa and The Royal Crescent Hotel all boast fantastic restaurants which have been making a big mark on the Bath food scene in recent years. For something a little more relaxed, you can settle down in a cosy pub for a comforting, hearty meal or try something a little more sophisticated at one of the Bath Pub Company pubs. There's really no better way to wash down a tasty meal than with a great drink. Try a local tipple like Honey's Midford Cider or a pint of Kettlesmith beer, you'll find both in pubs and bars across the city. If you're more of a spirit drinker then head to The Canary Gin Bar, the home of Bath Gin, and sample a classic G&T or even a cocktail.

The city of Bath has a long foodie history and afternoon tea is a tradition not to be missed, with many places providing different variations on the enduringly popular theme. With its grand columns, magnificent interior and ornate decoration, The Pump Room is a fantastic place to take afternoon tea. It truly embodies what was once the heart of the Georgian social scene, when high society flocked to Bath to 'take the waters'. Within The Pump Room you'll find the King's spring water fountain, where you can purchase a glass of the warm spa water to drink. This mineral-rich water has been used for curative and medical purposes for over 2,000 years.

Bath is home to two famous buns: the Sally Lunn bun and The Bath bun. The Sally Lunn bun is famous across the world and extremely popular with visitors. According to legend, Sally Lunn, a Huguenot refugee, arrived in Bath in 1680 and introduced a baker to her light, airy, brioche-style bun. It soon became popular at the public breakfasts and afternoon teas that were fashionable at the time. The recipe for the bun is still a closely guarded secret and is actually mentioned in the deeds of Sally Lunn's Historic Eating House and Museum, one of the oldest houses in Bath.

The Bath bun was invented by 18th century physician Dr William Oliver. The doctor's buns were originally made from a rich, sweet egg and butter dough topped with crushed caraway seed comfits. However, they were so tasty his patients' waistlines expanded at an alarming rate and they had to quickly be replaced with the far plainer, savoury Bath Oliver biscuit. Today's Bath bun is still made from sweet yeast dough - often with a whole sugar lump in the centre.

Bath and its surrounding area is a foodie heaven, with plenty of independent delis and producers, a local farmer's market and a strong community emphasis on locally sourced, home-grown food. If it's top quality meat you're after, head down to Larkhall Butchers, or if you're looking for something a little sweeter, Bath Cake Company have got you covered. The choices are endless.

Get stuck in to Bath and let us take you on a gastronomic tour of the city's best restaurants, cafés, pubs and producers!

Bathe in Bath and BEYOND

Tuck into Bath and you'll discover that one of the world's architectural masterpieces has a truly rich heritage.

Nestled in a sheltered valley and surrounded by lush countryside, Bath is nourished by natural hot springs which deliver the same thermal water harnessed by the Romans. Far from a museum piece, Bath is a modern city boasting a stunning 21st century spa complex – the only place in the UK where you can relax in natural thermal waters.

The golden city of Bath has been welcoming visitors for over 2,000 years. Designated by UNESCO as a World Heritage City, Bath presents some of the finest architectural sights in Europe and when visiting the city, architectural highlights such as the Royal Crescent, the Circus and Pulteney Bridge are not to be missed.

At the heart of the city, next to Bath Abbey, are the Roman Baths. Around one of Britain's naturally hot springs, the Romans built a magnificent temple and bathing complex that still flows with natural hot water; see the water's source and walk where Romans walked on the ancient stone pavements around the steaming pool. You can also 'taste the waters' which once attracted so many people to Bath. Head across the road and you'll discover the 21st century answer to the Roman Baths: the Thermae Bath Spa. Here, you can relax in the mineral-rich waters as the Romans and Celts once did thousands of years ago, but in a modern spa complex. The Spa's piece-de-resistance is its roof-top pool – open all year round – with stunning views of the surrounding cityscape.

If thermal waters aren't for you, take a meal and enjoy being serenaded with live classical music in the 18th-century Pump Room, a Georgian dining experience. The Romans aren't the only notable visitors of course, with Jane Austen once calling Bath her home. Two of her published novels, Northanger Abbey and Persuasion, are set in the beautiful city. She is celebrated every September with the Jane Austen Festival; a whole host of tours, recitals, day trips and Georgian themed activities take over the city.

Bath's vibrant food scene has not been built on the thermal water alone. Afternoon tea is also at the heart of Bath's culinary past. There is a mouth-watering selection of restaurants, pubs and tea shops on every street. Try a local delicacy, the Sally Lunn Bun, at the oldest house in Bath, still made to the original secret recipe or enjoy afternoon tea in one of Bath's traditional cafés.

Baked to PERFECTION

Whatever the occasion, Bath Cake Company can bake anything your taste buds desire. From custom cupcakes to truly show stopping cakes, Celia and her talented team have got you covered.

Celia Adams and her small team of five skilled bakers provide all manner of bespoke celebration cakes for any special event, from weddings and birthdays to anniversaries and hen parties. Working previously as a wedding planner, Celia knows how important a beautiful cake can be to making someone's day that bit more special. That's why she offers wedding cake consultations by appointment, to chat about ideas and do tasting sessions in the bakery's dedicated consultation room. Celia and her team are driven by their customers, dedicated to providing impeccable service and a truly personal experience that they won't receive anywhere else.

Celia first began baking with her mother at a young age and Bath Cake Company started life in Celia's own kitchen back in 2010. Selling her home-baked wares at Green Park Market proved popular and the need to re-locate to a permanent bricks and mortar shop quickly became apparent as the business grew.

Bath Cake Company is not your average bakery. Celia and her team don't just bake fabulous cakes, they also teach cake decorating classes at their very own decorating school, the only one of its kind in Bath. Try your hand at anything and everything from cupcake decorating, icing, modelling, stacking, chocolate work and making sugar flowers. Celia is PME approved to teach the internationally recognised PME Professional Diplomas and Masters Certificate, perfect for any budding baker to gain an official qualification for their skills or for someone looking to set up their own commercial baking business. Celia is also a 'Paul Bradford Sugarcraft School' Accredited Tutor, teaching a range of Paul Bradford's exciting cake decorating classes at the company bakery.

A Bath Cake Company cake has to look spectacular of course, but it's also got to taste incredible. The recipe overleaf for their maple and pecan chocolate drip cake ticks all of these boxes and it's a real favourite with the whole team. Indulgent and oh so decadent, this four layer cake is sure to be a crowd pleaser, whether you bake it for a family birthday or as an extra special teatime treat.

Bath Cake Company

MAPLE AND PECAN
CHOCOLATE DRIP CAKE

Delectably indulgent and oh so chocolatey, this drip cake will always be a winner! Get creative with your decoration to add a more personal touch.

Preparation time: 20 minutes | Cooking time: 1 hour 30 minutes | Makes one 4 layer 6" cake

Ingredients

For the cake:

7 eggs

350g golden caster sugar

350g self-raising flour

½ tsp baking powder

70g pecan nuts, chopped

350g unsalted butter, softened

For the buttercream:

175g butter, softened

450g icing sugar

1 tbsp whole milk

For the decoration:

250g dark chocolate

1 bag toffee popcorn

1 bag giant pretzels

100g whole pecans

Method

For the cake

Preheat the oven to 150°c.

Cream the butter and sugar together until lighter in colour.

Add the eggs one at a time with a spoonful of the flour and beat until smooth.

Gently fold in the remaining flour, baking powder and chopped pecans.

Split the mixture between four 6" round tins and bake for 35 minutes until the cakes are springy to touch and a skewer comes out clean.

For the buttercream

Beat all the ingredients together for 5 minutes in a mixer or with a handheld beater.

For the decoration

Once cooled, place your cake onto a cake board or plate.

Fill the cake in between each layer with buttercream using approximately one quarter between each layer of cake and saving approximately one quarter for the outside of the cake.

Once the cake is filled, spread the rest of the buttercream around the sides and over the top, then using a side scraper or palette knife scrape around the outside to create a semi-naked finish.

Chill in the fridge for 15-30 minutes.

Melt the chocolate in the microwave or over a bain-marie.

Pour the chocolate over the top of the cake and use a knife to encourage it to drip over the edge.

If there is any chocolate left over you can dip the pretzels in it.

Before the chocolate sets on the cake decorate with the pretzels, popcorn, pecans and anything else that takes your fancy!

A gin of a different
PERSUASION

Add a splash of creativity, a glug of eccentricity and a large measure of Jane Austen to a cocktail shaker and mix. Gin lovers and cocktail connoisseurs; drink up the elixir that is The Bath Gin Company.

The Canary Gin Bar, housed in a five storey Georgian building in the heart of Bath, is where the story began for The Bath Gin Company. Four years and ten select botanicals later and this Georgian gin palace is now home to Bath's first distillery for 250 years. Keeping the process, from infusion to bottling, well and truly in-house is bartender-come-head distiller Sam Travers. The flavour? Floral, citrusy and warm, modelled on Jane Austen herself who winks playfully from the label on the bottle. The key ingredient, and what makes Bath Gin so drinkable, is the Kaffir lime leaf. Added to the mixture at first as an after-thought, the lime leaf was the last piece of the botanical jigsaw and now forms a key part of the perfect serve, as a garnish.

As well as adorning the bottle, Jane Austen serves as the inspiration behind the company's International Brand Ambassador 'Virginia Gin Austen', who documents her daily life on Bath Gin's social media.

Brand manager Paul Bowring describes her as "Jane Austen's cheeky alter-ego." Anecdotes include: "I like to have a martini, two at the very most. After three I'm under the table!" (Dorothy Parker) and are always followed by a mischievous wink. Austen's personal connection with Bath is what inspired this clever and unique branding and it is from her novels that the cocktail menu comes alive.

The Canary Gin Bar itself is an intimate and candle lit affair spanning two floors. Its beautifully eccentric décor is the design of proprietor, former architect and artist Peter Meacock, who himself views the entire outfit as "one big art project" fashioned with merriment in mind. The first floor serves cocktails crafted by some of the city's most talented mixologists. Try their take on the classic Aviation, The Darcy, or if like so many you're more taken with Austen's most sparkling heroine Elizabeth Bennet, the Lizzy B, with champagne and lemon juice, is for you. Take a trip up the winding staircase and you'll find the Martini Bar where traditional tipples are distilled with an innovative modern twist. Join The Bath Gin Club here for regular gin tasting events and study mixology with the gin maestros themselves in a cocktail masterclass.

The opening of the Bath Gin laboratory in the basement of the bar means the future is infused with promise for The Bath Gin Company, with a new edition cucumber gin in the pipeline next.

The Bath Gin Co.
WICKHAM MULE
AND JANE'S GARDEN

George Wickham is a handsome man with 'a fine countenance, a good figure and very pleasing address.' One of Jane Austen's scoundrels, he had a fair kick. Bath Gin with Wormwood bitters and striking ginger beer gives the Wickham Mule a considerable flick in its tail.

The Janes Garden is inspired by Jane Austen's love of flowers and gardening; she took as much delight from her flower borders as she did from her kitchen garden. "You cannot imagine – it is not in human nature to imagine – what a nice walk we have round the orchard." Cucumber infused Bath Gin, apple juice and elderflower cordial, fennel bitters and lemon juice create a refreshing moreish complexity.

Ingredients

For the Wickham Mule:

Ice cubes

50ml Bath Gin

25ml fresh lime juice

5 drops Wormwood bitters

Ginger beer, to top

Kaffir lime leaf and slice of ginger, to garnish

For the Jane's Garden:

50ml Cucumber Bath Gin

50ml apple juice

20ml elderflower cordial

25ml fresh lemon juice

6 drops of fennel bitters

Cucumber slice, to garnish

Method

For the Wickham Mule

Place all the ingredients into a Collins glass.

Top up with ginger beer.

Drink up!

For the Jane's Garden

Place ingredients in a cocktail shaker and fill with ice.

Shake and fine strain into coupe glass.

In excellent COMPANY

For The Bath Pub Company, a great pub needs three key things: great food, great service and a friendly, welcoming atmosphere. They've achieved this with their four pubs, each with their own individual style, but with a shared commitment to high standards and quality service.

We start our tour of Bath's best gastropubs with The Chequers, tucked just behind The Circus and Royal Crescent. If you're after restaurant quality food in the relaxed environment of a pub, The Chequers is a must-visit. Winning both Best Sunday Lunch and Best Gastropub at the 2016 Bath Good Food Awards, The Chequers is a mainstay on the foodie map of Bath. If you can't decide between all the delectable options on offer, whet your appetite with the 7-course tasting menu; try a little bit of everything and discover your favourite.

Just down the road you'll find The Marlborough Tavern, the quintessential British gastropub, serving quality home-cooked food. With a cosy courtyard garden that is a real sun trap in the summer, the Marlborough is a hub for locals and tourists alike all year round. Hosting regular foodie tasting events and theme nights, The Marlborough has more than earned its two AA rosettes for culinary excellence.

Down by the canal is The Locksbrook Inn, the latest addition to The Bath Pub Company's portfolio. After a stylish refurbishment that is both modern but in keeping with the pub's long history, The Locksbrook is open daily from 8.30am, serving coffee in the mornings and brunch at the weekends. Don't be fooled though, with a dedicated bar area set apart from the restaurant, The Locksbrook is still very much a pub. The menu blends British classics with international twists, so there is something to satisfy every appetite and eating at The Locksbrook is truly a social affair, with a variety of dishes designed for sharing on offer.

The final stop on our journey is The Hare and Hounds, perched high on a hill overlooking Bath. With stunning views across the city and surrounding countryside, the location of this picturesque pub is pretty special, and so is the food. The menu is understated and unfussy, with the focus on pleasing customers with quality and taste. The Hare and Hounds is busy all day, serving breakfast from 8.30am right through to dinner. Whether you fancy a coffee with a view or a hearty lunch, there's something for everyone here.

The Chequers
HAY ASH VENISON WITH RED CABBAGE, PICKLED BRAMBLES AND HAZELNUT GNOCCHI

Cooking the venison in hay this way adds a deeper flavour to the meat.
Combined with the colours of the blackberries and the red cabbage, this is an
ideal dish for autumn.

Preparation time: Start preparing 24 hours in advance | Cooking time: 2 hours | Serves 4

Ingredients

For the venison:

1 loin of venison

1kg sweet meadow hay

For the red cabbage:

1 large red cabbage

750ml red wine

500ml Port

500g brown sugar

568ml orange juice

1 cinnamon stick

3 star anise

For the pickled brambles:

100ml apple juice

100ml raspberry vinegar

100g sugar

3 small punnets of blackberries

For the hazelnut gnocchi:

1kg desiree potatoes, baked and
scooped out of the skins

125g 00 pasta flour

2 eggs, yolks

100ml hazelnut oil

A handful of chopped hazelnuts

Knob of butter

Method

For the venison

Burn the hay with a blow torch until fully blackened, there should be no green visible at all.

Blitz the blackened hay in a food processor into a fine powder.

Dust and roll venison in the ash powder to evenly coat it.

Reserve the venison in the fridge until you're ready to cook it.

To cook

Roast the venison in a pan on a medium heat for 6 minutes on both sides. Remove from the heat and rest the meat for another 6 minutes, then carve and serve.

For the red cabbage

Shred the cabbage as finely as possible. Add this to a pan with all the other ingredients and cook on a medium heat until the cabbage is sticky.

For the pickled brambles

Add the apple juice, raspberry vinegar and sugar to a pan. Bring this mixture to the boil and then pour it over the blackberries. Reserve until ready to serve.

For the hazelnut gnocchi

Mix all ingredients together in a bowl while the potato is still warm.

Once the ingredients are thoroughly combined, roll into 25g balls and form into cylindrical shapes.

To cook the gnocchi, blanch it in salted boiling water until it floats.

Once cooked, add to a separate pan and toss in foaming butter to colour.

To serve

Plate the venison, red cabbage and gnocchi. Serve with the blackberries and a generous drizzle of the pickling liquor. You can also serve the dish with a few florets of broccoli.

Hare and Hounds

ROAST COD FILLET WITH CHORIZO AND BUTTER BEAN CASSOULET

This hearty dish makes the perfect lunch or light dinner.

Preparation time: 30 minutes | Cooking time: 1 hour | Serves 4

Ingredients

4 cod fillets

For the cassoulet:

2 celery sticks, diced into 1cm chunks

2 white onions, diced

3 garlic cloves, chopped

½ tsp smoked paprika

50ml vegetable or pomace oil

2 tins chopped tomatoes

50g tomato paste

2 tins butter beans

6 chorizo sausages, chopped into 1cm chunks

For the lemon, garlic and parsley dressing:

1 bunch of parsley, finely chopped

2 garlic cloves, diced

1 lemon, zest

50ml extra virgin olive oil

Salt

Method

For the cassoulet

In a heavy based pan, add the oil and warm to a moderate heat.

Add the chorizo pieces and cook out for 5 minutes until lightly coloured.

Add the onions, garlic and a pinch of salt and cook until soft

Add the smoked paprika and tomato paste. Cook for a further 5 minutes.

Add the tinned tomatoes and simmer on a low heat for 45 minutes to an hour, until the mixture has reduced by a third and thickened.

Drain the butter beans and add to the sauce. Heat through for 5 minutes and then leave to rest.

For the lemon, garlic and parsley dressing

In a small saucepan add the oil, lemon zest, garlic and a pinch of salt. Gently bring to a simmer.

Take away from the heat and allow to cool, then add the chopped parsley.

For the roast cod

Heat a non-stick pan and add a tablespoon of oil.

Season the cod fillet and place skin-side down in the pan. Sear on a high heat until the fish colours slightly.

Place in the oven and cook until the fish has gone firm and opaque.

Remove from the pan and allow to rest.

To serve

In a bowl, add a portion of the cassoulet and place the cod on top.

Drizzle the dressing over the cod and in and around the cassoulet.

Serve with a green salad.

The Marlborough Tavern

PAN-FRIED BRILL, PARMENTIER POTATOES, CAULIFLOWER TWO WAYS AND PICKLED FENNEL

Cauliflower is given a tasty pick-me-up here done two ways. An interesting take on a staple vegetable.

Preparation time: 1 hour | Cooking time: 40 minutes | Serves 4

Ingredients

4 brill fillets

1 large potato, chopped into small cubes

70g samphire

1 cauliflower

1 fennel bulb

570ml whole milk

For the pickling liquor:

150ml white wine

150ml white wine vinegar

150g caster sugar

5 pink peppercorns

2 bay leaves

1 tsp turmeric

2 shallots

For the lemon and coriander butter:

1 lemon, zest and juice

150g butter

30g coriander

For the tempura batter:

100g plain flour

50g cornflour

200ml soda water

Salt and white pepper

Method

For the pickling liquor

Put all the ingredients into a pan except the fennel and bring to the boil. Take off the stove to cool and then pass the liquid through a sieve. Finely slice the fennel bulb and place into the liquid.

When cool, place the mixture into a container and refrigerate.

For the cauliflower purée

Slice half the cauliflower and place in a pan with the whole milk, a pinch of salt and white pepper. Bring to the boil and leave to simmer until the cauliflower is soft.

When soft, pass the milk into a bowl and place the cauliflower into a food processor. Blitz with 2 tablespoons of the milk and a knob of butter until smooth then add salt and white pepper to taste.

For the coriander and lemon butter

Place all the ingredients in a food processor with a pinch of salt and blitz together to combine. Take the mixture out of the mixer and roll into a sausage shapes in cling film.

Place in the fridge to set.

For the parmentier potatoes

Place the potatoes in a pan of water and bring to the boil. Simmer for 5 minutes then drain and cool under cold water.

For the tempura battered cauliflower

Whisk together the ingredients for the batter and place in the fridge till needed.

Cut the remaining cauliflower into florets and fry in the batter in a pan of oil or deep fat fryer at 180°c for 2 minutes.

When the cauliflower is cooked, remove from the oil and season with salt and pepper.

For the brill

Preheat the oven to 180°c.

Cook the brill fillet skin-side down with the potatoes for 2 minutes, turning the potatoes constantly to colour on all sides. Place the pan in the oven for 4 minutes and start warming the cauliflower purée in a pan.

To serve

Remove the fish from the oven and serve on a plate with the puréed and battered cauliflower, a portion of samphire and two slices of the lemon and coriander butter.

Garnish with the pickled fennel.

The Locksbrook Inn

BANOFFEE

This dessert is essentially a classic banoffee pie deconstructed and updated for 2016, it looks great served in a kilner jar!

Preparation time: 20 minutes | Cooking time: 15 minutes | Serves 4

Ingredients

For the base:

50g butter

50g light muscovado sugar

397g condensed milk

For the topping:

110g mascarpone cheese

110ml crème fraîche

¼ tsp vanilla essence

25g icing sugar

For the garnish:

100g ginger biscuits, crushed

400g banana or vanilla ice cream

50g grated plain chocolate

Sliced confit stem ginger

For the salted caramel sauce:

200g granulated sugar

60ml water

55g salted butter (if using unsalted butter, add ½ tsp of fine sea salt or more to taste)

115g heavy cream

For the caramelised banana:

2 bananas

20g brown sugar

Method

For the base

Heat the butter and sugar gently in a large non-stick pan until the sugar has dissolved.

Add the condensed milk and stir with a flat ended wooden spatula, stirring continuously and evenly for about 5 minutes or until the mixture is a golden toffee colour and thick. Be careful, the mixture can burn easily.

For the topping

Tip: this cream makes a very versatile condiment. It is heavenly with fresh berries or roasted fruit.

Mix the mascarpone and crème fraîche with a tablespoon of sugar and the remaining vanilla essence. Stir it together really well.

For the salted caramel sauce

In a medium heavy-bottomed saucepan, stir together the sugar and water.

Bring to the boil over a high heat, stirring constantly until the sugar has dissolved.

Once the mixture reaches a boil, stop stirring and allow it to boil until it turns a deep amber colour but don't let it burn. As soon as the sauce has turned a dark amber colour, add the butter, keeping your face away from the pan, and whisk vigorously until the butter has melted and fully combined.

Stand back because the mixture will bubble up. Let it boil for another minute, remove it from the heat and carefully pour in the cream.

It will bubble up furiously again, be careful! Stir the mixture until it's fully combined. If you are using salt this is the time to add it.

Transfer the salted caramel sauce to a glass jar or a heat-safe container. Allow the sauce to cool uncovered at room temperature.

For the caramelised banana

Peel the bananas and cut into 10cm chunks.

Sprinkle with brown sugar and caramelise with a blow torch.

If you don't have a blow torch, you can caramelise the banana under a hot grill.

To assemble and serve

Serve this deconstructed banoffee pie in a medium-sized kilner jar, approximately 350ml in volume. Start by putting a layer of the caramel base into the bottom of the jar, and let it set. Top this with two pieces of the caramelised banana, followed by the mascarpone topping.

Garnish with the crushed ginger biscuits, salted caramel sauce and the grated chocolate. You can even add toffee popcorn, be creative with the garnish!

Serve with a portion of the ice cream and enjoy!

Cooking up a STORM

Whether you're popping in for a quick pint or on the lookout for a tasty meal, all are welcome at The Beaufort.

The Beaufort, located in Larkhall, is run by long-time friends Robbie Tack and Jack Scarterfield. Robbie heads up front of house, with his famous charm, and Jack is in charge of the kitchen. The pair have worked on many different ventures together over their 20 year friendship before taking on The Beaufort in 2015.

Offering fine dining in a relaxed atmosphere, the food at The Beaufort is all locally sourced. The menu changes weekly depending on what Jack can get his hands on, but you can guarantee there'll be some seafood on offer. The menu is always full of variety so dining at The Beaufort is never dull, with a mix of Asian flavours and British and European dishes. Favourites with regulars include the chicken Kiev stuffed with garlic, rosemary and lime butter and Jack's variations on Thai seafood curry. Their lamb shoulder madras is award-winning! Jack hasn't forgotten the vegetarians, and his Italian stuffed courgette flowers with ricotta are a real treat. Sunday lunches at The Beaufort are also a big hit, with regulars flocking for their famous roast Larkhall Butchers beef sirloin with all the trimmings. Jack truly lives and breathes cooking and this passion shines through in every dish. Nothing leaves his kitchen unless it's "spot on".

In order to make the most of their supplier's best produce, Jack cooks up monthly tasting menus including gluten-free and vegetarian feasts and 5 courses dedicated to game. This is just one of the reasons The Beaufort won 'Best Newcomer' at the Bath Good Food awards in 2015. Robbie and Jack are just getting started at The Beaufort, and they hope to win a lot more awards in the future!

You can try your hand at one of Jack's seafood recipes over the page; give his monkfish and octopus yellow curry a go. It's so simple to make but is packed full of flavour.

The Beaufort

GRILLED CORNISH MONKFISH AND OCTOPUS YELLOW CURRY WITH COCONUT RICE AND ASIAN SLAW

If you've never tried octopus, this exotic curry is perfect opportunity to try something different.

Preparation time: 2 hours | Cooking time: approx. 1 hour | Serves 4

Ingredients

4x200g trimmed monkish fillet

1 medium octopus, cleaned

Salt and pepper

Sunflower oil

For the rice:

340ml water

400g jasmine rice

2 tins coconut milk

For the sauce:

2 tins coconut milk

2 onions, chopped

1 red pepper, sliced

4 garlic cloves, chopped

1 thumb-sized piece fresh ginger, sliced

1 tbsp Thai yellow curry paste

1 tbsp Thai fish sauce

1 tbsp Thai fish sauce

For the slaw:

2 Thai chilli, chopped

1 tbsp palm sugar

1 tbsp Thai fish sauce

2 limes, juice and zest

1 green papaya, thinly sliced

3 heritage carrots, thinly sliced

To garnish:

1 handful Thai basil

½ bunch coriander

Method

To prepare the octopus

Cover the octopus in cold water and bring to the boil. Simmer for 1 and a half hours until tender and then remove from the water to cool.

For the rice

Wash the rice in cold water and pour into a heavy base saucepan. Cover with 2 tins of the coconut milk and the water. Stir thoroughly and bring to a simmer.

Cook slowly for 20-25 minutes until all the liquid has gone.

For the sauce

Fry the onions, peppers, garlic and ginger until tender. Add the Thai yellow paste, the 2 remaining tins of coconut milk, 1 tablespoon of fish sauce and 1 tablespoon of palm sugar. Cook for 30 minutes on a medium heat.

For the slaw

Peel the carrots and green papaya and then thinly slice. For the dressing, mix the lime zest and juice with 1 tablespoon of fish sauce, 1 tablespoon of palm sugar and 2 chopped Thai chillies.

To cook the fish

Preheat the oven to 200°c. Heat up a griddle pan and season the monkfish with salt, pepper and sunflower oil. Grill both sides until golden then roast in the oven for 6 minutes.

Remove the tentacles from the octopus and grill for 2 minutes each side.

To serve

Spoon the coconut rice into individual serving bowls. Pour over the yellow curry sauce, slice the monkfish and place on top. Add 2 tentacles of the octopus and add the Asian slaw.

Sprinkle with the Thai basil and coriander.

Wandering, but NOT LOST

Beth Al-Rikabi AKA The Free-range Chef learnt that saying yes to things that scared her was the only way to grow.

The dictionary definition of free-range refers to "natural conditions" and "freedom of movement"; no phrase embodies Beth and her business better. Falling into cooking entirely by chance, Beth now cooks in kitchens from Italy and Morocco to Ibiza to markets, pop-ups and supper clubs in the West Country.

After working in kitchens across Bath, Beth set up her own business Beth's Bakes in 2008, creating all kinds of quirky cakes. When asked if she could bake something, her response was always that she'd give it a try. It is this can-do attitude that is the most striking thing about Beth and her business, and it has enabled her to expand: "I realised I had too many ideas to work for someone else, I had to go out on my own."

Whilst freelancing with FareShare South Wests' Surplus Supper club, Beth got her first taste of catering for a large number of people. This experience also highlighted the massive issues surrounding food waste: "It forced me to think differently and be more creative by using seasonal produce." The next test: cooking at a yoga retreat in Italy for three months. It is here that the 'Free-range Chef' was born and Beth realised that she needed to say yes to any opportunity that came her way, no matter how anxious it made her. "It's all gone crazy since then!" she laughs.

Pure passion for organic ingredients and cooking sustainably is what drives Beth to keep experimenting with food. This commitment to ethical produce and vegetarian food however does not necessarily mean all her creations are conventionally 'healthy', as she explains: "I'm not going to hold back on the salt, butter and good stuff if it makes the food tastier! The best way I know to make people happy is to feed them good food."

Variety is the spice of life and no two adventures are ever the same for The Free-range Chef. Learning early on to adapt to unique situations and stay calm when problems arise is the key to her success. One particular experience sticks out: "I was cooking for a wedding breakfast for 40 in a domestic kitchen in Mykonos which involved preparing 12kg of very rustic lamb and 12kg of fresh octopus. The slimy fellows were rather overwhelming! But it turned out tasty in the end!"

Now, when faced with any new challenge, Beth's first thought is always: "At least it's not 12kg of octopus!"

THE FREE RANGE CHEF

~Markets~Wedding Cakes~
~Pop Up Events~Food Writer~
~Retreat Chef~Mindful Munch Catering~
Fulfilling by Need to Eat

THINK Happy

RO

THE
ROMAN BATHS

A taste of FRANCE

Be transported to South West France at The Bunch of Grapes, the perfect neighbourhood bar restaurant serving rustic French classics in Bradford on Avon.

The Bunch of Grapes is a collaboration between five friends with one thing in common – another life spent amid the vineyards of south west France, cooking, eating and drinking. Andrew and Anna Barwick own and run Chateau Rigaud near Bordeaux and together with head chef Steve Carss and friends Debrah Smith and Peter Woodcock, they're bringing all the best bits of south west France to the UK.

Arriving back in the UK with a team of eight from the chateau, the staff at The Grapes are incredibly passionate about what they do. Head chef and co-owner Steven Carss has been with the team for seven years, having initially trained under Rick Stein. Their classic French dishes are often cooked traditionally in the 'Bertha' wood fired oven, which burns oak, ash and a variety of fruit woods every lunch and dinner service. If you walk by in the evening you'll be greeted by its warm glow and comforting scent. The pissaladière, wood fired flat breads served with salad, make an excellent lunchtime snack. Try the moules frites, which are fast gaining a reputation, inspired by the famous Chez Hortense in Cap Ferret where they add chorizo and ham to the mix. The rest is a closely guarded secret!

What truly makes The Bunch of Grapes special is their wine selection. The team imports their wine directly from small scale producers in south west France, there are no wholesalers or distributors involved at all. This means there is no mark-up, and each bottle is personally selected. Peter even assisted in the harvest of the Oiseau! If you love the wine as much as the team and want to enjoy it at home, it's also available to purchase by the bottle at the chateaux prices. The Grapes also serve expertly curated cocktails, crafted seasonally by the bar team Cameron and Phil.

The Bunch of Grapes isn't just about bringing the best food from France; the team want you to truly experience eating in a French village bar bistro. That's why most of the décor has been brought in from across the channel, with quirky wooden plaques and prints adorning the walls. The whole space, perfectly lit by Tom Dixon designer lighting, has that authentic French 'brocantes' feel.

The Bunch of Grapes

SOY CURED SALMON IN A CUCUMBER CUP WITH MANGO SALSA & WASABI CRÈME FRAÎCHE

This truly delicious canapé will wow your guests. It's beautiful to look at and super tasty. You can prepare every element in advance; keep the cucumber bases in water in the fridge until you're ready to assemble.

Preparation time: 15 minutes, plus 24 hours marinating | Makes 10

Ingredients

For the base:

1 cucumber

For the salsa:

½ mango

½ red onion

Chives, small bunch

1 tsp cider vinegar

1 tsp olive oil

Salt

For the marinade:

250ml soy sauce

150g soft brown sugar

1 piece ginger, 5cm

400g salmon, cut into 2cm strips

1 bunch coriander stalks

For the wasabi crème fraîche:

¼ tsp wasabi paste

1 tbsp crème fraîche

Method

24 hours before your party place the salmon in a small plastic box with the marinade ingredients.

Ensure the salmon is entirely submerged.

After 24 hours the salmon will be cured by the soy and is ready for use.

Cut the salmon into 1cm cubes.

For the salsa

Cut the mango and red onion into cubes and chop the chives. Mix through the cider vinegar and olive oil. Season to taste.

Cut the ends off of the cucumber and divide it whole into 2cm slices, place in water in the fridge.

Take a pastry cutter, just smaller than the circumference of the slice, and use this to remove the peel, leaving a perfectly round slice.

Use a melon baller to scoop out the centre of the slice creating a cup.

Mix the wasabi paste and crème fraîche together and put into a piping bag.

Take the cucumber bases from the water and stand on a clean tea towel to dry them.

Spoon a teaspoon of salsa into the cup, pipe on a dab of crème fraîche and position a cube of salmon on the top.

Tip

The leftover cucumber skin is great as a gin and tonic garnish!

Fat Fowl
PAN FRIED HAKE FILLET WITH CRAB
& CHORIZO RISOTTO & SALSA VERDE

Finn Young first worked at the Fat Fowl part-time when he was just 16, now
he's the head chef. Serving classic English food with a bit of a twist, the menu
at the Fat Fowl takes its inspiration from a variety of sources.
After spending some time travelling Europe over the summer, visiting France,
Italy, Germany, Belgium and Holland, Finn returned full of fresh ideas and
ready to experiment.
The team at the Fat Fowl are very proud of the independent food scene in
Bradford on Avon, and to showcase and celebrate this they're holding a food
festival which they hope will become an annual event!

Preparation time: 20 minutes | Cooking time: 30 minutes | Serves 4

Ingredients

4x140g hake fillet

Flour, for dusting

For the risotto:

350g risotto rice

2 shallots, finely diced

200ml white wine

150g butter

1 litre fish stock

350g white crab meat

90g Parmesan

325g chorizo, peeled and sliced

Salt

1 lemon, juice

For the salsa verde:

2 tbsp sherry vinegar

200ml rapeseed oil

2 tbsp parsley, finely chopped

2 tbsp tarragon

2 garlic cloves, crushed

40g capers, finely chopped

Pea shoots

Method

For the risotto

Heat 50g of the butter in a large saucepan.

Add the shallots and chorizo and sweat, stirring for about 2 minutes until the shallots are
soft and translucent.

Stir in the rice and cook for a further 2 minutes.

Add the wine and simmer, stirring constantly.

Add the stock slowly, allowing the liquid to be absorbed before adding more. This process
can take around 15 minutes.

Add the crab, Parmesan and 40g of butter.

Add the lemon juice and salt to taste.

For the hake

Heat the remaining butter in a pan.

Dust the hake with flour and fry skin-side down for 3-4 minutes until the skin has become
crisp, then turn over and cook for a further minute.

For the salsa verde

Mix together all the salsa verde ingredients.

To serve

Plate the risotto and top with the hake, skin-side up. Drizzle with the salsa verde and
garnish with pea shoots.

Fat Fowl

Updated CLASSIC

After spending thirteen years at the award-winning Tollgate Inn in Holt, Alison Ward-Baptiste and Alex Venables have given The George at Woolley a new lease of life.

Alison and Alex make a formidable team. With head chef Alex in charge of the kitchen and Alison heading up front-of-house, The George at Woolley, near Bradford on Avon is a pub on the rise. After taking over in March 2015, Alison and Alex gutted and then re-modelled the entire building almost entirely themselves, creating their traditional, old world inn from the ground up.

After pouring their heart and soul into reviving the pub, customers can trust the team at The George to provide the best of everything. The kitchen is completely open plan, meaning diners can watch Alex and his team work their magic on each course. After previously enjoying Michelin-star status at country house hotel Lucknam Park, Alex knows a thing or two about cooking excellent food. The menu at The George changes almost daily depending what is available – you can guarantee there will be some game, and everything is homemade on site, it's not unknown for the occasional squirrel pie to feature! Homemade cakes are always featured on their daily display and are all lovingly designed and created by senior pastry chef Grace. Community spirit is high at the inn and locals and regulars often bring in their own produce for Alex to cook up, in exchange for a meal. "Traditional, proper grub but stylishly served", Alison explains the team aren't into food fads and trends. Diners will always get a delicious, hearty meal at this pub!

The George is far more than just another country pub; Alison and the team aim to offer something that bit different and special to their patrons. The George holds a regular Saturday morning cookery school, where the chefs share their extensive knowledge, teaching eager customers everything from making fresh pasta and bread to properly preparing and cooking game. If you're looking to improve your home cooking, pop by and brush up on your skills! The team also hold regular themed gourmet evenings every eight weeks, which are very popular with diners new and old. There is always something going on at The George and Christmas is no exception! Keen to support their community, Alison and the team run a Christmas market where local artists' work is displayed for purchase. Everything from paintings to sculpture, glassware and pottery can be found on sale, perfect for picking up a unique Christmas gift.

In keeping with tradition, the upstairs of The George houses two luxury self-contained apartments, aptly named Thyme and Rosemary. If you're simply having too much fun to leave, why not stay the night?

The George

PAN FRIED VENISON WITH A HUNTERS PIE ON A BED OF SAVOY CABBAGE AND BACON

This dish makes use of what's available in the local Woolley countryside.
The perfect hearty meal for a chilly winter's dinner.

Preparation time: 3 hours | Cooking time: 30 minutes | Serves 1

Ingredients

For the hunters pie:

150g venison leg, cubed

150g mushrooms, sliced

60g onions, chopped

30g garlic, chopped

4 tbsp parsley, chopped

60ml dry red wine

30ml red wine vinegar

200ml beef stock

20g olive oil

200g mashed potato

50g grated cheese

Salt and pepper

For the venison:

225g venison loin, trimmed

200g Savoy cabbage, blanched

50g streaky bacon, cut into strips

For the marinade:

2 garlic cloves

Juniper berries

100ml red wine

Method

For the venison

Add the venison to the marinade of red wine, garlic and juniper berries, cover and chill in the fridge for 3 hours.

For the pie

Heat the olive oil in a large frying pan and sear the venison cubes until they are brown. Once they are brown, remove them from the pan and put to one side.

Add the garlic, onions and mushrooms and cook until they are golden brown.

Add the red wine vinegar and reduce the mixture by half. Then add the red wine and reduce by half again. Add the beef stock to the reduction.

Add the venison cubes, parsley, salt and pepper and bring to a simmer.

Reduce the heat from medium to low and cover the pan until the venison is tender, this will take around 2 hours.

When cooked through, add to a small ramekin and top with mashed potato and grated cheese. Finish in the oven for 10 minutes.

To cook the venison

Take the venison out of the marinade and pat dry.

Pan fry the venison loin until evenly brown to seal the meat. Then cook in the oven for 8 minutes until medium rare.

Rest the meat for 10 minutes before serving.

To assemble and serve

Sweat the streaky bacon in a hot pan, try not to add colour to it and add the savoy cabbage. Add a little a splash of stock or white wine and a knob of butter and reduce.

The hunters pie should be cooked in the oven until the hat is bubbling on top.

Place the savoy cabbage and bacon on the plate first and slice the venison, placing it on top.

Serve the pie alongside.

Growing SUCCESS

Situated on the old naval base Royal Arthur Park, The Greenhouse is a stylish and relaxed all day dining destination with a difference. Located in an elegant and contemporary setting at the heart of Wadswick Green, with beautiful views across the Wiltshire countryside.

The Greenhouse Restaurant at Wadswick Green is open daily to residents and locals alike from 9am, serving light breakfasts, cakes and locally brewed coffee. The restaurant itself is visually stunning, with floor to ceiling panoramic windows providing an abundance of light to the open-plan space. Mixing shabby-chic furniture with modern and sophisticated fittings, The Greenhouse is a beautiful venue whatever the occasion. In the summer, dine alfresco on the patio or cosy up by the fire during the cold winter months.

The highly trained staff at The Greenhouse are quick to attend to guests needs and make it their priority to get to know regular customers. Friendly staff combined with impeccable service keeps diners returning to the restaurant. The Greenhouse offers a regular calendar of events so there's never a dull moment and whether you're visiting for a long lunch with friends or celebrating a birthday, the menu has something for everyone. No matter how adventurous your taste buds are, there will be something that will interest and excite you, inspired by home-grown British dishes or distant Mediterranean cultures. Try the chickpea, tomato and sweet potato curry for something with a kick or a traditional wood-fired pizza for a taste of Italy. If you're fancying something more classically comforting like a delicious burger or perfectly battered, good quality fresh fish, The Greenhouse has got you covered. The specials on offer daily are always highly seasonal and give the chefs an opportunity to demonstrate their range of expertise.

The bar is incredibly well supplied, with a carefully selected and extensive wine list. For wine lovers, The Greenhouse is like coming home: "We have a passion for great grapes and we're well-stocked too with tried-and-true favourites from crisp, refreshing white Pinots and Sauvignons and rosés to classic, juicy Riojas and Merlots, whether by the bottle or the glass." explains Penny Scambler, sales and marketing director. Thursday night is prosecco night at The Greenhouse, a very popular night with women in particular! With a bottle of prosecco priced at only £14.95 all night it's easy to see why!

The Greenhouse
MACKEREL BRANDADE

Enjoy this brandade as a light lunch, served with a chilled glass of Pinot Grigio.

Preparation time: 20 minutes | Cooking time: 20 minutes | Serves 4

Ingredients

150g smoked mackerel

100g potatoes

½ small chilli

½ shallot

20g coriander

1 lime, juiced

50ml extra virgin olive oil

Sea salt

1 loaf crusty bread, sliced

20g frisée lettuce

Method

Peel and chop the potatoes before boiling and mashing. Set them aside to cool.

While the potatoes are cooking, fillet the mackerel, take the skin off and remove all the bones.

Finely dice the shallot, chilli and coriander and mix them all in a bowl.

Mash up the mackerel with a fork and combine with the chopped ingredients. Add this mixture to the room temperature mash potato and season with lime juice, olive oil and sea salt to taste.

Toast the slices of crusty bread under the grill until golden.

Serve the brandade with the toast and the frisée lettuce.

Your rural FOOD HUB

Hartley Farm has been farmed by the Bowles family for five generations. Now, in 2016, it is much more than your average farm.

Hartley Farm, with its farm shop and café-kitchen is under the care of Tom Bowles, fifth generation farmer. Despite the precarious future of the farming industry, Tom wanted to join the family business in 2007 and help carve a new future for the farm. With his parents Richard and Kim, who had farmed at Hartley since the 1970s, Hartley Farm Shop opened its doors in 2008. Tom saw the need to diversify, combining his passion for farming and food to open the shop and café.

The farm's main activity is now beef production, which supplies the in-house butchers counter and in turn the farm kitchen, ensuring 100 percent traceability of all the animals from the farm to the shop. As well as a herd of Aberdeen Angus cattle, Hartley Farm is also home to a community of young, artisan businesses including a microbrewery, florist and sourdough bakery. Hartley Farm also welcomed market gardener Kate Collyns to their family in 2010, who supplies the farm shop with her fruit and vegetables as well as the wholesale trade. Tom explains: "The farm has become a local food hub, where a community of producers all make and grow things together."

The kitchen is where all of this passion culminates. The menu changes regularly to reflect what's in season, with a daily specials board. The food offering is never your usual run-of-the-mill café food however, designed to excite and inspire diners with hearty home-cooking to more adventurous dishes from around the world. The café also hold regular monthly supper clubs and food demonstration evenings collaborating with local chefs and cooks. At Hartley Farm, food is at the centre of everything. It's about sharing and connecting with people.

The business started with five members of staff and now the team is 70 strong, all with a shared passion and commitment to quality food and ingredients. Hartley Farm aim to provide something more to the customer than just a place to grab a quick coffee. However, if you do fancy a coffee, you can be sure it'll taste great because it's brewed right on site by José Melim and his team at Easy José Coffee.

In 2015 Hartley Farm opened a sister site, Neston Farm Shop and Kitchen, on the beautiful Neston Park Estate, near Corsham. Tom explains: "When the opportunity came to grow we felt strongly that it was an opportunity to try to develop our core purpose and values as a business in a new community. It's an exciting time for our business and for the local food industry, as interests and concerns surrounding health, lifestyle and education are coming into sharp focus. Our plan is to stay at the forefront of this and continue to grow with our community."

Hartley Farm
CHILLI, LIME AND CORIANDER SPATCHCOCK CHICKEN, JALAPEÑO CORNBREAD, WITH AN AVOCADO AND TOMATO SALSA

Serve this spicy chicken at the table so your family or guests can help themselves.

Preparation time: 20 minutes, plus 12 hours marinating | Cooking time 1 hour 15 minutes | Serves 4

Ingredients

1 whole chicken

For the chicken marinade:

2 red chillies, 1 green chilli

1 tbsp sweet paprika

2 limes, zest and juice

2 tbsp runny honey

4 spring onions

1 tsp allspice

1 small handful oregano

1 small handful thyme

4 garlic cloves

80ml olive oil

For the cornbread:

125g plain flour

125g cornmeal

60g light brown sugar

100g cheddar cheese, grated

3 tsp salt

3 tsp baking powder

235ml buttermilk

1 egg

2 jalapeño chillies, finely sliced

For the salsa:

4 tomatoes, roughly diced

2 avocados, roughly diced

1 red onion, thick diced

1 handful fresh coriander, chopped

2 limes, juice

80ml extra virgin olive oil

Salt and pepper, to taste

Method

For the chicken

Preheat the oven to 180°c.

To spatchcock the chicken, place it breast side down on a chopping board. Use kitchen scissors to cut along each side of the excess fat at the bottom of the chicken and either side of the backbone.

Discard the backbone and turn over the chicken; push down on the breastbone to flatten it. Cut several deep slashes in each leg joint and set aside.

Put all the ingredients for the marinade in a food processor and blitz to a paste.

Rub into the chicken and marinade for at least 12 hours or overnight.

Place the chicken on a roasting tray and cook for 50 minutes.

For the cornbread

Preheat the oven to 200°c and grease a square baking dish.

Mix together all the dry ingredients.

Whisk the egg and buttermilk together and then stir into the dry ingredients mixture.

Pour into the baking dish and sprinkle the sliced chillies on top.

Place in the oven and cook for 20 minutes, until golden brown and springy to the touch.

For the salsa

Mix all the ingredients in a salad bowl and season.

Serve with a lime wedge and tuck in.

We are FAMILY

Honey's Midford Cider began as an experiment and soon blossomed into a successful commercial operation.

As with many of the best stories, it all started in the pub. Local farmer Bob Honey saw a small advert for an 18th century cider press in a farming magazine and inspiration struck. The Honey family have farmed in Midford for over 60 years and the old maps of the land – like so many in Somerset – had "orchard" marked on several grass paddocks. Deciding to continue the tradition, Bob, his daughter Jules, son-in-law Krow and a bunch of other residents set about making cider from local windfalls one weekend a year. It was less about the cider - which was undrinkable in the early days - and more about a group of family and friends having a good time making it.

As the years passed, the cider got better and Honey's Midford Cider gradually turned into the booming business it is today, supplying a wide variety of restaurants, pubs and bars locally and customers as far away as Hong Kong! However the majority of Honey and Daughter cider is sold within six miles of the cider press and made with traditional Somerset cider apples, a truly provincial drink.

Keeping tradition alive is important to Honey and Daughter. They've revived the historic Somerset drink known as Stoney Bonk, a magical blend of cider and ginger beer, and now sell it bottled along with their classic craft cider. It's a real winner; both as a thirst-quenching drink in the summer and a welcome warming kick come winter. Born and bred in Bath, community spirit is very much thriving in both Bob and Krow, who have become involved in the re-opening the Packhorse Inn in South Stoke, along with 200 other community investors. Honey and Daughter will of course by supplying this much-loved pub with their cider come spring 2017.

The Midford farm is now dedicated both to rearing beef and growing apples for the cider, joint enterprises that complement each other perfectly. The cattle graze under the trees and provide fertility to the orchard soil, and then each autumn they're fed the leftover apple pomace once the juice has been pressed. It's this kind of sustainable business that makes Honey and Daughter so special. Jules and Krow have two daughters that have been brought up with the farm as their second home, now the fourth generation of Honeys in Midford. Perhaps one day Honey and Daughter will become Honey, Daughter and Granddaughter!

Get your FIX

The In A Pickle kitchen is located in the beautiful village of Winsley, just 5 miles from Bath city centre, but you can find their products throughout the UK and into Europe.

As a professionally trained chef, when Steph Anderson saw fresh ingredients going to waste right in front of her, she had to do something about it. After raiding a neighbour's garden for fruit from their trees and making chutney to sell at her son's school Christmas Fair, In A Pickle was born.

Five years later and Steph now works in a purpose built kitchen with a small team to bring her unique recipes to life. Everything is still handmade though, as it was at the very beginning. All of the In A Pickle and In A Jam products are personally invented and taste tested by Steph and the team so they can be sure customers are getting the very best. While the business may have grown exponentially since that first batch was sold at her son's school, Steph has made sure the company values have not changed.

From the signature In A Pickle Lily to the Moroccan inspired Lemon and Apricot chutney, you can be sure whatever jar you choose will be spot on and full to bursting with taste. Steph and the team pride themselves on their unique and unusual flavours, which often draw inspiration from around the world. Creating traditional chutneys and jams with authentic oriental and Indian spices is what sets In A Pickle

apart from the pack. Steph says: "Creating new recipes and products is like taking a culinary spice journey around the world. I'll order the spices and when they arrive it is interesting to see that they have come from all corners of the globe." The team at In A Pickle are also keen to update and re-vamp the conventional way chutney is used by suggesting new ways to eat them, rather than just as a traditional accompaniment to a cheese board or meat platter. Try their sweet chilli jam as a dipping sauce for prawns or roll up their lemon and apricot chutney inside a lamb shoulder before slow roasting. You can even use it as a baste before BBQing.

In A Pickle has won numerous awards throughout the years, including Great Taste Awards for their Hot Lime Chutney and In A Pickle Lily as well as several Taste of the West Awards. Steph and the team are also incredibly proud to have won both the Bath Good Food and Bristol Good Food Award for 'Best Local Condiment' for the past several years. She explains: "Bath is a real foodie community with a whole host of amazing artisan producers so it's really great to know we've been singled out."

In A Pickle
ST STEPHEN'S PIE

This is a firm Christmas tradition in the In A Pickle household. It's a delicious way to use up leftover turkey and the end result is a combination of crisp golden pastry and a rich, creamy filling. Our special Christmas chutney adds a hint of cranberry sharpness.

Preparation time: 20 minutes | Cooking time: 40 minutes | Serves 8

Ingredients

8 tbsp mayonnaise

2 tsp Dijon mustard

450g leftover turkey, chopped into pieces

120g Gruyère or cheddar cheese, grated

2 celery sticks, chopped

85g sweetened dried cranberries

2 sheets ready rolled puff pastry, chilled

8 tsp In A Pickle Christmas chutney

Black pepper, freshly ground

1 egg

Chopped walnuts, to top the pie

Flour

Method

Preheat the oven to 200°c.

To make the filling, measure out the mayonnaise and Dijon mustard into a large bowl and mix together.

Add the turkey, cheese, celery and cranberries and bind together. If necessary add a little more mayonnaise to get a dropping consistency.

Unroll one sheet of puff pastry onto a flat baking tray and top with the filling, leaving a clear border about an inch wide around the edge.

Drop the chutney onto the filling at regular intervals; the pie will later be cut into 8 portions so place the chutney accordingly.

Crack the egg into a small bowl and beat with a fork, then brush around the edges of the pastry (save the rest to do the top of the pie).

Unroll and lay out the second sheet of pastry onto a lightly floured board, and fold loosely in half, long sides together, and cut from the folded side towards the edge, leaving an inch border all the way round, so that you end up with slits across the middle of the sheet once unfolded.

Lay this sheet of pastry over the top of the filling and press the edges down to seal.

Brush the top of the pie with the remaining egg wash and sprinkle with the chopped walnuts and a little pepper.

Bake for 40 minutes, until the pie is golden brown.

Serve with a green salad, and some more Christmas chutney on the side.

Variations

Swap the turkey for chicken, swap the Gruyère for cheddar cheese, swap the celery for spring onions or swap the Christmas chutney for In a Pickle sweet chilli jam and omit the cranberries.

Cultivating CHANGE

Jamie's Farm aims to transform the lives of disadvantaged children. They provide a unique combination of 'farming, family and therapy' through a short stay residential and follow up programme. Aiming to re-engage children with educational life, and enable them to flourish both in school and the wider social setting.

During their visit to Jamie's Farm, children participate in a range of therapeutic activities including farming, horticulture, horse-work, carpentry, art, log chopping, and of course cooking. These activities are set in the calm, beautiful countryside of Wiltshire and Herefordshire, and give the children the chance to succeed in meaningful jobs, boosting their self-esteem and enabling them to see themselves and the world around them in a new, more positive light. They aim for children to return to school re-energised and inspired about the opportunities available to them and the positive paths that their life can take.

"Food has the potential to open our minds to new and wonderful experiences. It enables us to share our cultures, develop our creativity and build confidence. Food forms a major part of the week at Jamie's Farm. The children are involved in every aspect of it, including the growing of fruit and vegetables, caring for the livestock, butchery, food preparation and serving. At Jamie's Farm we try to give children the chance to experience a healthy diet full of great food, much of which is familiar, some of which is new, all of which is delicious." Said Rob Lewis, farm food and events manager.

Many of the young people who visit the farm have diets that are high in sugar, salt and other ingredients common in processed and fast food. This has a number of negative health implications both physically and mentally, and can result in behaviour counter to the best versions of themselves. By eating a healthy diet, low in these ingredients, many of the young people who have visited the farm have been transformed, both in the colour in their faces and in the calmness of their demeanour. This change occurs in the space of just a few days.

"Despite the negative impacts of a poor diet, we try not to be preachy about food, or tell children what they should or shouldn't eat. Instead we try to influence diets by making healthy food fun to make, beautiful to look at, and wonderful to eat." Adds Robert

Joy, creativity, provenance and seasonality are at the core of all their food. The cooking sessions start with a trip to the garden where they look to see what is growing and hand-pick the produce before taking it back to the barn, where they decide what to make. This helps to give children a better understanding of where their food comes from, links their diet to the seasons, and makes for fresher, tastier meals.

Jamie's Farm

PUFF PASTRY PIE WITH AUBERGINE, TOMATO AND MOZZARELLA

"This plaited pie looks great and is very versatile; you can really play around with fillings. At the Farm we try to use whatever is in season and growing in the garden. This aubergine and mozzarella combo is so tasty, sings of summer and uses aubergines and tomatoes from the polytunnel as well as homemade mozzarella using milk from our own jersey cow."

Preparation time: 25 minutes | Cooking time: 30 minutes | Serves 8

Ingredients

1 sheet ready rolled puff pastry 30x40cm (or a 500g block rolled into a rectangle the thickness of a pound coin)

2 large aubergines, cut into 2cm cubes

2 garlic cloves, finely chopped

6 large tomatoes, roughly chopped (or use a tin of chopped tomatoes)

Small handful basil, chopped

2 handfuls mozzarella, grated

Olive oil

1 egg, beaten

Salt

Method

Preheat the oven to 220°c.

In a large frying pan, heat a large glug of olive oil over a medium heat and fry the aubergine ensuring that you do not overcrowd the pan.

Cook until the aubergine is golden and cooked through (it will become very soft). You will need to do this in several batches. Drain the aubergine on some kitchen roll to absorb some of the excess oil.

Once you have cooked the aubergine, fry the garlic for about one minute until it is just taking on some colour before adding the tomatoes. Add a large pinch of salt and cook for ten minutes to reduce.

Add the aubergine and the basil, and take off the heat whilst preparing the pastry.

Tear a sheet of baking parchment slightly larger than the pastry and place the pastry on top. Divide the pastry into thirds lengthways marking very faintly with a knife. Now cut the two outer segments into strips 3cm thick. Lift the parchment and pastry onto a large baking tray.

Now add the tomato and aubergine mixture along the centre of the pastry leaving about 5cm at either end uncovered. Sprinkle the cheese on top of the mixture.

Bring the ends of the pastry over your mixture and then bring up the strips you have cut into the centre, one at a time, alternating between sides to create a plaited effect (you can use a bit of egg wash to aid the sticking process). Try to avoid leaving any large gaps or your mixture may fall out. If you have any excess pastry you can cut this into strips and use it to patch up any holes.

Brush the beaten egg mixture all over the pie and bake in the oven for 25-30 minutes until golden brown. Leave for five minutes before slicing with a serrated knife and serving.

Re-think the way YOU DRINK

Only brewing since May 2016, you are invited to explore the world of beer with Kettlesmith...

Kettlesmith Brewing Company are trying to change the way people see beer. Spearheaded by head brewer and Certified Cicerone Antony Field, the team at Kettlesmith believe beer has a place in restaurants and at the dinner table, as an alternative to wine.

This way of thinking comes from Antony's background as a homebrewer living in San Francisco, California. Antony explains: "The market is so much more mature in the US, beer is taken more seriously and we want this to happen in the UK." Antony is a Certified Cicerone, which took months of training, including courses at the Siebel Institute in Chicago. The title 'Cicerone' is to beer what 'sommelier' is to wine; it means those with the title have proven expertise in all aspects of beer, including brewing and serving.

Kettlesmith currently brew six signature beers, each with their own unique flavour and tasting notes as well as one-off and seasonal beers. Taking influence from Belgian and American beers, Kettlesmith put their own British spin on them, and the branding, much like the beer, is uncomplicated. Instead of adding to the noise and overwhelming drinkers, Kettlesmith are solely focussing on their product, and making the best possible beer they can. While they are keen not to bombard drinkers with too much information, the team do provide drinkers with intelligent food pairings, so you can get the most out of your Kettlesmith beer. Try their hoppy pale ale Faultline with chicken or vegetable curry or the Belgian pale ale Fogline with grilled pork.

Kettlesmith Brewing Company is still very young, but they've been two years of solid hard work in the making after nearly a decade of planning. At this early stage, Antony and the team are concentrating on "getting it right": making sure each and every bottle, cask and keg is perfect. Their goal is to be able to interact with drinkers and customers more through brewery open days and pop-ups, to educate them about the beer and encourage them to re-think the way they drink. Learning and adapting as they go, Kettlesmith Brewery are on the up, exploring the wide world of beer from Bradford on Avon.

A cut above
THE REST

There has been a butcher in Larkhall since before anyone can remember, and when Peter Milton took over the store in October 2015, he was continuing a long tradition.

Peter Milton took a Saturday job at Larkhall Butchers when he was just 12 years old, and now at 24 he owns the business. Growing up on a farm nearby, top quality, local food has always been a part of his life. Peter learned the butchery trade inside out at Larkhall, taking on more responsibility and enrolling for more training courses as the years went on.

Larkhall Butchers has won the title of 'Best Local Butcher' in the Bath Good Food Awards every year since the awards began, and Peter's aim is simply to maintain this high quality and where possible, to improve upon it. Larkhall is more than just your average butchers; they also sell fresh fish, their own charcuterie and a variety of deli products including their own honey.

At Larkhall, the team want to offer customers more of what they're looking for and something they cannot get anywhere else. One speciality product they are very proud of is their dry-aged beef. Dry-aging is a traditional process whereby beef is stored on the bone, without protective packaging, at low refrigeration temperatures. This process results in improved tenderness and the development of the unique flavour that can only be described as 'dry-aged beef'.

No other butcher in Bath currently offers this kind of beef; dry-aging takes considerable space, time and care to both perfect the conditions required in the refrigerator and store for the required time.

Local produce is important to the ethos of Larkhall Butchers and Peter has introduced one local producer in particular to the shop: children's charity Jamie's Farm, who take disadvantaged inner city children and give them the opportunity to work on a real farm. Growing up and helping out on his own farm, he knows how valuable those experiences can be: "The farm is only five minutes away from our shop and the meat is excellent, I really couldn't be happier to be supporting them."

The team at Larkhall Butchers are more than willing to go above and beyond for their customers, from bespoke joints to weird and wonderful cuts of meat. All you need to do is ask! Price is also crucial: because supermarkets offer such a limited range of fresh meat, most people aren't even aware of the affordable, lesser-known cuts that are value for money but still incredibly tasty. Pop in to the butchers and the team will be more than happy to help!

Larkhall Butchers
STEAK TARTARE GRATIN

This recipe is by Ma Cuisine, a family catering business situated in the heart of Larkhallm, across the road from the butchers. Head chef Cristophe prepares authentic gourmet French meals using local ingredients, fast-frozen to give you handmade meals with no additives or preservatives.
For more details about Ma Cuisine find them online at www.macuisine.co.uk.
This is their twist on the traditional steak tartare and features grilled cheese on top. But be careful, it's important when cooking the cheese not to cook the meat too.

Preparation time: 10 minutes | Cooking time: 2-3 minutes | Serves 2

Ingredients

280g beef sirloin, fat off

2 eggs, yolks

2 tsp shallots, finely chopped

2 tsp fine capers

1 tsp curly parsley, chopped

1 tsp tomato ketchup

1 tsp Dijon mustard

1 tbsp tabasco sauce

1 tbsp Worcestershire sauce

Salt and pepper to taste

50g Emmental cheese or vintage Cheddar, grated or finely shaved

Method

First, finely chop the sirloin with a knife, or ask your butcher to mince it for you.

Mix the sirloin with all the other ingredients listed, apart from the cheese. Save this for topping.

Add the salt and pepper to taste.

Using a circular shape cutter or by hand, shape the mixture into a large patty shape.

Top the patty with the chosen cheese and place it all under hot grill. Alternatively grill it with a blow torch until the cheese is golden.

Chef's tip

Do not leave the steak to stand for too long under the grill as you do not want it to cook.

To serve

Serve with a mixed leaf salad and crusty bread.

You've got a
FRIEND IN ME

With a lot of help and support from her family and friends, Elaine Lauga opened Mes Amis over a decade ago, and it's become a real institution in the village that her family have made their home.

In the quiet Somerset village of Beckington, you'll find Mes Amis at its beating heart on the main High Street. Mes Amis is incredibly popular, with delicious food, attention to detail and the 'extra mile' service it's easy to see why.

Beckington is a tiny community. It was first mentioned in The Domesday Book and became important in the middle ages for its connections to the wool trade. The location of the shop has always been a permanent fixture in the village, in the early years as a village Co-op and then later years as a gift shop. When the shop looked in danger of closing, Elaine knew she had to act to maintain a continuation of some form of commerce in its footprint. Building on her many years of experience in the hospitality business, working for Relais et Châteaux properties and some of the best 5-star establishments in the country, Mes Amis became her next project. Being married to a Frenchman, the concept was to create a French style charcuterie/traiteur whilst retaining an element of the gift shop the building had previously been known for. Within the first few weeks of opening, Elaine's neighbours and customers began donating tables and chairs because they wanted to stay on site to enjoy the atmosphere and food. She took the hint and applied for a 'change of use' for the premises and the rest is history!

The menu at Mes Amis is seasonal and regularly changes to reflect what's fresh and available locally. The talented team inject a "drizzle of loveliness" into all that they do, the menu is a very visual display of colours and flavours and pride of place is the famous spicy carrot salad that cannot be removed from the selection for fear of customer ramification. The team cook up and deliver an array of tempting tarts, a Plat Du Jour, frittatas and focaccia to complement the salads. The cake counter groans under a calorie laden display of temptations and delicious treats.

Elaine says: "We all feel so privileged here at Mes Amis to have shared in so many of our customer's lives over the last decade and truly value their loyalty and custom." Our daily routine can involve shared tears, laughter and excitement and every day is a new adventure."

MES AMIS

Come In WE'RE OPEN

Mes Amis
Opening Times
Monday - Saturday
9 - 5

Mes Amis

THREE CHEESE MUFFINS WITH PEA, SWEET CHILLI AND MINT DIP

The chefs at Mes Amis love variety and putting their own spin on a dish. This recipe lends itself well to creativity: try adding a medley of different flavours from grated courgette to smoky bacon.

Preparation time: 10 minutes | Cooking time: 12 minutes | Makes 12 large muffins

Ingredients

For the muffins:

75g parsley, roughly chopped

310g self-raising flour or gluten-free self-raising flour

150g mature cheddar, grated

65g Parmesan, grated

1 tsp salt

2 tsp ground black pepper

1 egg

315ml milk

80g butter, melted

Optional extras: a handful of grated carrot or beetroot, chopped rocket, courgette, chopped bacon or sun blush tomatoes. These can be added with the dry ingredients.

For the dip:

300g cream cheese

500g peas, cooked

2 tbsp sweet chilli sauce

80g fresh mint, to taste

2 garlic cloves

1 lemon, zest and juice

Salt and pepper, to taste

1 small red onion, finely diced

Pea tendrils, nasturtium flowers or nigella seeds, to garnish

Method

For the muffins

Preheat the oven to 180°c.

Mix all the dry ingredients together and the pour in the egg, milk and butter.

Stir quickly to form a lumpy batter; do not be tempted to over beat as the muffins will become heavy.

Grease the muffin tins and spoon in, dividing the mixture equally.

Bake for 20 minutes until golden brown.

For the dip

Blend together all the ingredients except the garnish and red onion with a hand blender until smooth.

Stir the red onion into the mixture.

To serve

Serve the muffins with a generous dollop of the dip and garnish with the pea tendrils, nasturtium flowers or nigella seeds.

Rising STAR

After winning 'The Publican's National Turnaround Pub of the Year' at the Great British Pub Awards 2012, The Methuen Arms has gone from strength to strength.

Located in the picturesque market town of Corsham, right next door to the stately home and stunning 'Capability Brown' landscaped grounds of Corsham Court, The Methuen Arms is steeped in history. The building itself dates back to the 14th century, and in 1799 ownership passed to the Methuen family who converted it to a coaching inn with stables. Fast-forward to 2011 and Martin and Debbie Still took the reins, transforming the derelict interior into the multi award -winning business it is today.

Martin and Debbie are very proud of their inn's heritage; The Methuen Arms has played a small part in every period of history since its building 700 years ago. Notably, the Duke of Edinburgh used to play skittles and darts here with the locals and his compatriots from the Royal Arthur Petty Officer Training School in Westwells. He also kept his sports car in the garage at The Methuen. He was courting Princess - now Queen - Elizabeth at this time, and is known to have asked his Commanding Officer for leave so that he could go to London and propose.

The Methuen Arms is a very popular venue, where taste and not trends lead the menu. Head chef Piero Boi is dedicated to preparing quality food that represents the fantastic produce readily available locally, including a wide variety of game. Everything is made on site, from bread and chutney to ice cream. This means Piero can be totally flexible in his cooking and personalise dishes around diner's diets and allergies. His nose to tail approach to food works well both for traditional pub fare and complex dishes. Provenance is incredibly important to Piero and his team, they like to know everything about the produce and meat they use to ensure it's up to par. The Methuen Arms has more than earned its two AA rosettes and foodies travel from afar to sample the great food.

The rosettes are not the only award The Methuen has won. Their bedrooms are rated 5-star by the AA and The Good Pub Guide awarded them The Best Dining Pub in Wiltshire accolade for 2016. They're also featured in The Good Hotel Guide and The Michelin Guide. It's been a busy five years, and there are big plans in store for the next 12 months!

The Methuen Arms

CHARGRILLED LAMB RUMP WITH STUFFED TOMATO, BORLOTTI BEANS, ONION SQUASH, GREEN OLIVES

"This dish was one that I cooked very early on in my career whilst working in London, and under the direction of the River Café's head chef Darren Simpson."

Preparation time: 20 minutes | Cooking time: 30 minutes | Serves 2

Ingredients

340g lamb rump, trimmed

160g fresh borlotti beans

80g onion or butternut squash

1 plum tomato, skinned and deseeded

2 anchovy fillets, chopped

8 sprigs rosemary

6 garlic cloves (or as much as desired for taste)

40ml lamb jus

20g Parma ham

20g green olives

2 red onions, diced

20g Parmesan

100g fresh white breadcrumbs

1 lemon, zest

10g flat parsley, chopped

2 carrots

2 celery sticks

2 sprigs thyme

Chilli flakes

Salt and pepper, to season

Rainbow chard or cavolo nero

Method

Preheat the oven to 180°c.

Season the lamb rump with salt and pepper and seal off in a hot pan. Once sealed, add 1 clove of garlic and 2 rosemary sprigs.

Place in the oven for 12 minutes. Take it out of the oven and leave to rest for 8 minutes.

For the stuffed tomato

Preheat the oven to 180°c. Sweat the Parma ham with the red onion and 1 clove of garlic.

Mix the breadcrumbs, Parmesan and the sweated ham with the lemon zest and season.

Blanch the tomato and remove the skin and seeds. Fill it with the breadcrumb mixture and bake for 10 minutes.

For the cavolo nero and borlotti beans

Pick the cavolo nero leaves from the stalk and blanch in boiling salted water until the leaves become tender.

Then, with the borlotti beans, cook together in water with the carrots, celery and onion until soft. Peel the squash if using and pan roast with garlic, chilli flakes and thyme.

Sweat down the borlotti beans and cavolo nero in chilli and garlic.

To serve

Warm the borlotti beans and plate. Place the tomato on top of the beans with cavolo nero and squash. Slice the lamb on top.

Take the lamb jus and add the chopped anchovy, rosemary sprigs and thinly sliced garlic. Bring to the boil and sauce over.

Chef's tips

Marinade the lamb the day before if you have time in rosemary, oregano, garlic and chilli. Alternatively, you could cook in a water bath at 58°c for 1 hour.

New Macdonald had A FARM

New Macdonalds Farm is located right on the outskirts of Bath. Their mission is to educate people on the provenance of their food and encourage them to seek out the very best produce they can find: high quality and grown with love.

Matt and Louise Macdonald are first generation rare-breed farmers, falling into the trade entirely by chance almost eight years ago. When Matt's friend broke his leg and needed some help on his dairy farm, Matt discovered his passion for cattle farming and decided a career change was in order.

Both Louise and Matt are originally from London, but they always knew they'd end up moving away from the big city, as Louise explains: "We knew we didn't want to raise our children in London, and when the land became available we thought it was time to give it a go." As a vegetarian, Louise has always been interested in animal welfare and Matt is a real foodie with an appetite for good quality, local produce; the pair complement each other perfectly.

The ethos at New Macdonalds Farm is simple: happy animals produce better quality products. Louise and Matt specialise in high welfare rare-breed meat and eggs. Everything they produce is of the very finest quality, from their pork to their speciality 'Quattro-Coloured' hens eggs. The Macdonald's guarantee each box of these high-nutrient eggs will contain at least four different coloured shells, a delight for the eyes and the taste buds! The eggs are so popular with customers that Louise and Matt can only just keep up with the demand.

Less than 3 percent of British pork is outdoor reared, but Louise and Matt pride themselves on being a part of this minority. Using old traditional farming methods, their Gloucester old spot pigs are slow-grown for 9 to 14 months and are fed premium food to ensure the meat is the best it can be. Every animal on the Macdonald's farm is outdoor free-range and enjoys fresh air, sunshine, grass and everything else Mother Nature has to offer. This kind of sustainable farming practice is what sets Louise and Matt apart. They truly care about their animals and the environment in which they live.

The Macdonalds take on a new project every year and Matt has big plans for 2017 and beyond, looking to go back to their roots and get some pedigree cattle back on the farm such as the Hereford or Ruby Red breed. It's important to Louise and Matt to support rare-breed animals that are in critical danger of dying out, and with this in mind they are looking to take on some British Landrace pigs. Whatever challenges come their way, it's always onwards and upwards for New Macdonalds Farm!

Where history meets THE MODERN

Tucked away in the village of Chilcompton, only a stone's throw from Bath, The Redan Inn is a historic pub.

The Redan Inn has been newly refurbished by the team behind The Pumphouse in Bristol and The Bird in Hand in Long Ashton. They have extensively restored the inn, with seven lavish boutique bedrooms now ready to welcome guests.

A traditional inn, with the bar open all day, all week, The Redan has lots of home comforts. From the rolling garden and sofa decked terrace outside so guests can take advantage of the summer sunshine, and a roaring wood-burner to keep things cosy when the weather turns colder, The Redan is the perfect setting whatever the weather. The bar always has a host of treats on offer, from ever-changing local ales to over 100 gins each with their own unique serves and garnishes and an extensive wine list for all occasions; the drinks roll with the seasons here as much as the food does.

Situated in a glorious location for local produce, head chef Tony Casey and his team revel in blending his experience of modern cooking styles with the very best ingredients sourced from right on their doorstep. The kitchen is supplied by local farmers and growers, as well as foraging the rich Mendip countryside and daily deliveries from the coast; the team are dedicated to finding seasonal perfection in all they cook up. They also have the luxury of their own kitchen garden, growing an assorted plethora of goodies just outside the door. Whether it's one of their renowned breakfasts, a light bite from the lunchtime bar menu, the à la carte menu, or a more decadent tasting menu in the private dining room, expect the chefs to enthusiastically create both traditional pub classics and intriguingly different dishes with a touch of flair.

Indulgence is the order of the day when it comes to their bedrooms, from the duvet and pillows to the bath products and towels, everything is well thought out and designed with ultimate comfort in mind. Each of the seven rooms all have wonderful unique, period features and are decorated with vintage and antique furniture and artwork. They are completed, of course, with quirks from co-owner Dan's legendary collection of curios and trinkets: new, old and even older. Every room has its own feel and story.

The Redan Inn

RAW AND PICKLED BEETROOT, TRUFFLED GOAT'S CHEESE, HAY ASH

From beautiful heritage beetroot with their incredible range of colours, to the familiar deep purple ones, they are a joy to cook with as they are so versatile. This recipe lets loose a variety of textures and techniques; sure to be both great fun to prepare and a wow factor for everyone eating it.

Preparation time: 2 hours | Cooking time: 1 hour | Serves 4

Ingredients

Salt baked beetroot:

12 beetroots (4 red, 4 golden, 4 candied)

Rock salt, enough to cover

For the raw and pickled beetroot:

1 red, 1 golden 1 candied beetroot, thinly sliced

500ml water

500ml white wine vinegar

500ml sugar

5 cloves

2 star anise

1 tsp coriander seeds

For the beetroot purée:

300g salt baked beetroot (as above)

500ml apple juice

75ml Port

50g sugar

1 orange, juice

Salt

For the goat's cheese mousse:

250g goat's cheese

1 tsp truffle oil

75ml double cream

For the hay ash:

50g hay

To garnish:

6 radishes, sliced

Black onion seeds

Micro herbs

Beetroot powder

Toasted hazelnuts

Method

For the salt baked beetroot

Preheat the oven to 180°c. Wash the beetroot to remove any dirt.

Line a baking tray with foil and cover with a layer of rock salt. Place the whole beetroot on top, wrap and cover with foil. Cook in the oven for 1 hour 15 minutes.

Once the beetroot is cooked, peel it and set aside 300g for the purée. Cut the remaining beetroot into circles.

For the purée

Take the 300g of the beetroot that has been set aside and cut into 1cm chunks.

Place in a pan along with the Port, apple juice and sugar. Cook until the liquid has reduced by two thirds. Squeeze in the fresh orange juice and place in a blender, blitz until smooth.

Season with salt and pass through a sieve. Leave to cool, and store in the fridge until needed.

For the pickled beetroot

Heat the liquids and spices with the sugar until the sugar has fully dissolved. Set aside to cool and divide equal amounts into three containers.

Thinly slice the beetroot using a circular cutter, cut out circles from the beetroot slices. Place each different colour beetroot into the 3 separate containers of the now cooled pickling liquor.

The pickling can be done a few days in advance and kept in the fridge to add more flavour.

For the goat's cheese mousse

Blend the cheese in a food processor with the truffle oil.

Slowly add the cream until fully combined, but be careful not to over-whip the mixture.

Roll into 2cm diameter balls and leave to set in the fridge.

For the hay ash

Burn the hay to cinders, using a blow torch. Cool, sieve, then store in a container.

To serve

Place the pickled beetroot on the plate and dot the purée in between.

Lightly roll the goat's cheese in the hay ash and add.

Slice the radishes and place on the plate along with the hazelnuts.

To garnish, sprinkle with the seeds, beetroot powder and a selection of micro herbs.

When in FROME

The River House café opened its doors at Christmas in 2014. In just two years it's become a thriving destination for locals and after extending it's opening hours, The River House is now far more than just your average café.

The River House is the brainchild of local 'Fromian' Ellen Porteous. After eating and drinking her way around the country, Ellen was inspired to open her own venue closer to home in Frome where she could "kip at mum and dad's and have her washing done for free". Enlisting the help of Frome's finest food fanatics - with a shared passion for eating and drinking and more eating and more drinking - The River House is now known for its obscure menus, excellent coffee and varied bar which includes craft ales and fabulous cocktails.

Situated on a bridge overlooking the River Frome, The River House is a three-storey building with great views. The small but friendly café is decked out in an individual style, with hand-crafted tables, blackboard murals and graphic design details; an interesting place for people to meet and chill out. The River House is open 7 days a week for breakfast, brunch, lunch and of course coffee. The passionate and coffee-mad team, headed up by barista extraordinaire Olly, are part of the reason customers become regulars. That, and the great coffee they serve. Supplied by local, ethical roasters Dusty Ape, The River House's coffee is unrivalled in Frome. In fact, the team are so coffee-mad that they're in the process of opening up their own in-house roastery to offer customers a new and unique blend.

Tuesday to Saturday The River House serve an evening menu until 9pm and the same love and care they apply to their coffee goes into the food. Head chef Pascale Vickery works with the team to serve up the most on-trend brekkies and brunches, whilst creating an ever-changing seasonal evening menu of small plates; small but packed with flavour. The bar's range of craft beers and inventive cocktails make The River House a top evening destination. Try their mainstay Espresso Martini if you like your coffee with a kick, only as good as the espresso it's made with! No fear though, The River House's boozy brunches are legendary: dynamite food served with a Bloody Mary, they are known to ward off even the most potent of hangovers.

The River House
CRAB TOAST WITH HERB AIOLI

Indulge in this decadent dish, perfect as a starter when entertaining guests, or even as a posh lunch when you feel like treating yourself.

Preparation time: 15 minutes | Cooking time: 15 minutes | Serves 6

Ingredients

For the herb aioli:

4 egg yolks

4 garlic cloves, roasted

250ml vegetable oil

250ml olive oil

50ml lemon juice

2 tsp salt

1 tsp cracked pepper

Small handful dill

Small handful parsley

For the crab:

1 lemon, cut into 6 wedges

300g white crab meat, cooked

1 cucumber, peeled into ribbons

6 slices sourdough

Olive oil to rub

To serve:

Red vein sorrel, red amaranth, black pepper

Method

In a large bowl whisk the egg yolks briefly, add the garlic and beat in.

Slowly drizzle in the vegetable oil, whisking thoroughly. Do not allow the mixture to split.

Whisk in the lemon juice and slowly drizzle in the olive oil, whisking thoroughly.

If the aioli starts to become too thick, add a small amount of water gradually.

Finish seasoning with salt and pepper to taste, then folding through the chopped parsley and dill.

Drizzle the sourdough with oil and grill until toasted.

Mix the prepared aioli with the crab to the desired consistency.

Lightly fold through the cucumber ribbons, season and top onto the sourdough

Top with the micro herbs, black pepper and serve with a lemon wedge.

On top of the
WORLD

When the most iconic hotel in Bath took on a chef who'd cooked the England rugby team to World Cup glory, it was no surprise it made for a winning combination.

David Campbell, executive head chef at the 3AA Rosette Dower House Restaurant at The Royal Crescent Hotel and Spa, is someone who is used to being part of a winning team. A former chef for the British Lions and England rugby team, he was a part of the backroom staff that travelled to Australia in 2003 and came back with the World Cup.

David moved to The Royal Crescent Hotel and Spa in 2010 to take up the role of executive head chef, which was a difficult time for the business. David takes up the story:

"When I took on the role at the hotel, I knew I had a large mountain to climb to get to where we wanted to be, the restaurant at the time was under previous ownership and had gone from 3 AA rosettes to 2 and the business was in administration. Topland Group thankfully came in during 2012 and totally refurbished the hotel, building us a new kitchen along the way. And with general manager Jonathan Stapleton starting in 2014, we now have a renewed purpose and a real sense of direction."

Situated on one of the most famous crescents in the UK, the five-star hotel is not only one of the most iconic buildings in Bath but also one of the best examples of Regency architecture you'll find anywhere in the world. Designed by

famous Georgian architect John Wood the Younger, the hotel consists of 45 suites and rooms, fabulous walled gardens, The Spa and Bath House as well as the restaurant and a fabulous champagne and cocktail bar.

Like the hotel itself, the menu in The Dower House restaurant has evolved over recent years, and David feels it now showcases the self-belief he has in his cooking.

"Food needs to look good, taste good and eat well," he says. "My style has actually got simpler over the years. I think as you become more confident in your flavours and techniques you learn to say 'that's enough'. If you look at the really great chefs in this country; Sat Bains, Phil Howard, Daniel Clifford, Jason Atherton etc. they are all in their 40s and have got that experience to not only be a better cook but a more confident one, as well as a better manager."

As David points out, the hotel is classic in style but they run a modern service and the food reflects that. It means that each guest will enjoy a variety of experiences here; whether you're staying on site and looking for a reasonably-priced lunch or afternoon tea, or you're after a seven course taster menu for a special occasion, David and his team have it covered.

The Royal Crescent Hotel
HAY SMOKED SALMON, CAULIFLOWER, RADISH AND LEMON

Chef's tip: "This recipe looks simple, but deceptively so, there are quite a lot of components to pull together so you need to be well organised and precise."

Preparation time: 1 hour | Cooking time: 45 minutes | Serves 4

Ingredients

For the salmon:

1 side Loch Duarte salmon, skinned, trimmed and pin boned

250g Maldon sea salt

250g caster sugar

1 lemon, zest

Hay

Rock salt, to smoke

For the cauliflower:

½ cauliflower, trimmed to florets

300ml milk

100ml double cream

½ bay leaf

Salt and pepper, to taste

Knob of butter, for cooking

For the lemon:

3 whole lemons

Stock syrup, to blanch the lemon

For the radish:

3 breakfast radish

Method

For the salmon

Skin the salmon, remove any brown fat, trim neatly and ensure all pin bones are removed.

Mix the sea salt and sugar together well and zest the lemon into this mixure. In a tray, pack this mixture onto both sides of the salmon evenly and allow to sit at room temperature for 30 minutes, this firms up the salmon, cures it and seasons it at the same time.

Wash off the sugar and salt mix under cold water, pat dry on a cloth and transfer to sous vide bag. Cook in sous vide bath at 40°c for 24 minutes. Alternatively, steam the salmon. Chill in the bag in an ice bath.

To smoke the salmon, remove it from the bag and place on a steamer tray. Wrap the tray tightly in cling film, three layers should be enough. Place the hay and some rock salt in a separate tray. Blow torch and then quickly drop the tray with the salmon on top, this extinguishes any flames and causes smoke to form, leave the tray with salmon on top for 10 minutes to take on a smoke flavour.

For the cauliflower purée

Sweat ¾ of the florets in a sauté pan with butter, add the bay leaf and season with salt and pepper. When the florets are just starting to cook add the milk and double cream. Cook on a high heat for 15 minutes or until the florets are soft.

Drain the cauliflower but keep the cooking liquid. Transfer to a food processor and blitz on high. Add the liquid slowly back in until the mixture is smooth and shiny, the consistency should be a similar thickness to custard. Chill and reserve.

For the cauliflower florets

Pick some small florets, only one or two, and break them down in to mini florets the size of your small fingernail. Blanch in boiling water for 30 seconds, drain and refresh.

For the raw cauliflower

Cut two florets from the cauliflower and slice these down thinly with mandolin. Reserve.

For the lemon

Peel a lemon carefully, just remove the yellow outer skin, don't get the pith! Blanch the lemon zest for 1 hour on a very low heat in the stock syrup with the juice of another lemon and set aside. Completely peel the first lemon to just leave the flesh. Segment this neatly, remove any pips, and place in a little stock syrup with lemon juice to balance. Reserve.

To serve

Cut a piece of salmon approximately 1½ inches width and plate. Place 4-5 dots of the cauliflower purée carefully on top, add some mini florets, some of the lemon segments and then the raw cauliflower slices. Garnish with a few strands of the lemon zest and a few slivers of radish. Drizzle a tiny bit of smoked oil and rock salt on top. Place a generous blob of the pureé next to the salmon.

Written in the
STARS

Originally an 18th century farmhouse, The Seven Stars should traditionally be named 'The Plough' to reflect it's history, however since there are already two pubs in the surrounding area with this name, The Seven Stars is named after the constellation of stars that represent the plough in the night sky. The success of this country pub is literally written in the stars...

The Seven Stars pub in Winsley ticks all the boxes: good food and great service in a warm and welcoming atmosphere. This traditional country pub has had many owners in recent years, each with their own ideas regarding the key focus of trade. When Kate and James Hooper took over in 2015, their main goal was to place the pub back in the heart of the community, catering as best they could for all their customers.

They've made this happen through sheer hard work, dedication and team work. From the kitchen to the front of house staff, the close-knit team at The Seven Stars are the driving force bringing this country pub eatery back to life. There is nothing customers appreciate more than excellent service and friendly staff, something which the front of house staff at The Seven Stars are constantly praised for. Their passion, pride and professionalism is infectious.

Head chef James and his kitchen staff are devoted to cooking top quality, hearty food using local and seasonal produce from the neighbouring Hartley Farm. Everything is homemade,

from freshly baked bread to a range of ice creams. The menu changes frequently and the recent addition of a gluten-free menu has proved extremely successful. Kate explains: "We have recently embraced the demand for gluten-free options, and are one of the few restaurants in our area that can now offer a plethora of dishes free from gluten. This includes fish and chips and sticky toffee pudding, rare treats for a celiac, but only a fraction of what we can offer our customers bound to such dietary requirements."

As part of their vision to rebuild the community reputation of the pub, the team at The Seven Stars hosted their first family fun day and festival over the summer, providing live music, children's entertainment and delicious homemade BBQ food. The event was set up to raise money for the local school and pre-school; community spirit at its peak! The event was so successful that Kate and James have plans to make it an annual fixture.

The Seven Stars

FILLET OF BEEF WITH BEETROOT PURÉE, DAUPHINOISE POTATOES AND A RED WINE AND PORT REDUCTION

This classic dish is perfect for a dinner party, focus on cooking the beef well and it'll taste great!

Preparation time: 30 minutes | Cooking time: 1 hour 30 minutes | Serves 4

Ingredients

4 beef fillet steaks

3 large beetroot

8 asparagus spears

4 whole baby corn

For the dauphinoise potatoes:

8 large potatoes, thinly sliced

280ml cream

3 garlic cloves

1 sprig thyme

Salt and pepper to season

For the sauce:

430ml beef stock

175ml red wine

50ml Port

Salt and pepper to season

Juices from the cooked fillet

Method

Preheat the oven to 160°c.

For the dauphinoise potatoes

Put the cream in a saucepan with the thyme and garlic and bring to the boil. When the mixture is boiling, remove it from the heat and keep to one side to infuse for about 15 minutes. Once the cream has infused, strain through a sieve.

Layer the potatoes in a tray or gratin dish, season and pour the infused cream over each layer until it's all used up.

Put a layer of greaseproof paper and then tin foil over the top of the tray and cook in the oven for approximately 1 hour or until soft. Near to the end of the cooking time, remove the greaseproof paper and tin foil and turn the heat up to 180°c to brown the top.

For the beetroot purée

Bring a saucepan of water to the boil, add the beetroots and simmer until soft. Once the beetroot is cooked, strain the water from them using a colander. Put the beetroot into a food processor and blend until smooth.

Season the purée with salt and pepper.

For the sauce

Pour the red wine and Port into a saucepan and reduce by half over a moderate heat. Add the beef stock and reduce again by half or until the mixture has thickened.

Season with salt and pepper to taste.

To cook the beef

Heat a splash of oil in a hot frying pan. Cook the fillet steaks in the frying pan for about 6-8 minutes, turning a few times to brown all over. Once the beef is cooked, remove it from the pan and leave it to rest for about 5 minutes.

Pour the juices left from frying pan into the red wine and Port sauce.

To cook the vegetables

Bring a saucepan of hot water to the boil.

Put the asparagus and baby corn into water and blanch for no longer than 2 minutes.

Serve the beef fillet steaks with a portion of dauphinoise potatoes, beetroot purée, asparagus, and baby corn on a plate and pour some of the red wine and Port sauce over the top.

The right ingredients
FOR SUCCESS

Bath College has run catering and hospitality courses for over 30 years and is a big part of the local food scene of the city; training Bath's future chefs and front of house staff is something they've perfected.

Some of Bath's best young chefs both learn and work at the busy Shrubbery Restaurant, serving delicious three-course menus to lunchtime diners. The restaurant, right in the heart of Bath on James Street West, is a bright and modern venue popular with locals and students alike. Each and every dish is prepared, served and cooked by students studying catering and hospitality at the college, using only fresh, seasonal ingredients. The menu evolves with the curriculum and is changed weekly, featuring both international and modern British cuisine.

Thanks to the college's well-established reputation in the city, bookings for the Shrubbery Restaurant's regular evening themed dinners are quick to fill up, with past events including a St George's Day Dinner and a Mardi Gras Dinner. Last year, the students hosted an imaginative 80th birthday banquet, serving eight courses inspired by popular dishes throughout the decades. Being a chef and running a restaurant is not just about how well you cook, it requires a huge amount of creativity and the college's themed events encourage students to utilise all of their skills.

The alumni of Bath College go on to do great things, working at Michelin-starred and AA Rosette restaurants across the West of England; notably, the talented Andre Garret at Cliveden House Hotel and Stuart Ash at Woods in Bath. To provide their students with the very best career opportunities, the college has established a hotel and restaurant school, linking students with the top establishments in the city and giving them a chance to experience real life working in a prestigious kitchen.

You don't have to be a student to go and learn something different; the college offers a wide range of part-time courses for adults, from Italian and Vietnamese cookery to cake decoration and bread making. If you fancy a taste of something new or want to brush up on old skills, Bath College is the ideal place.

The Shrubbery
ICED APPLE PARFAIT WITH CALVADOS

This boozy parfait makes a perfect dinner party dessert.

Preparation time: 30 minutes, plus 12 hours setting time | Cooking time: 20 minutes | Makes 12 portions

Ingredients

For the parfait:

350ml double cream

4 eggs yolks

100g caster sugar

75ml water

3 cooking apples, puréed with sugar and lemon juice

1 gelatine leaf, soaked in cold water

50ml Calvados

For the brandy snap:

115g butter

228g caster sugar

115g golden syrup

115g soft flour

1 tsp ground ginger

For the salted caramel sauce:

450g double cream

300g light muscovado sugar

90g unsalted butter

2-3 pinches sea salt

Method

For the parfait

Line a 7cm pastry ring for each portion with an acetate strip or baking parchment and place in the freezer.

Place the sugar and water into a thick-bottomed saucepan. Cook until the mixture is 121°c or has formed a soft ball.

Whisk the cream until it is holding shape. Whisk the egg yolks, then pour in a stream of the cooked sugar and whisk until cool.

Warm the Calvados gently and add the softened gelatine. Add this to the egg mixture.

Add the egg mixture into the purée of apple and fold in the whipped cream. Pour the mixture into the lined pastry ring and freeze. Take them out 15 minutes prior to serving.

For the brandy snap

Preheat the oven to 180°c.

Cream the butter, sugar and golden syrup together and add the flour and ground ginger.

Form into a soft paste and roll into a sausage shape between silicone paper. Chill in the fridge.

Shape into small sticks about 15cm in length, place onto baking parchment and bake in the oven for 12 minutes. Tap the tray during the baking to allow the mixture to spread.

Shape while still hot by cutting into a strip 2cm wide, then form around the outside edge of the pastry hoop. Allow to cool.

For the sauce

Place the cream, sugar and butter in a medium sized, thick-bottom saucepan.

Gently heat this mixture, stirring continuously until the sugar has dissolved and the butter has melted.

Bring to the boil and simmer for 3-4 minutes until thickened and smooth.

Cool slightly and taste the sauce. Add the salt sparingly to taste.

Pour into a plastic sauce bottle and pipe a bulb onto your service plate. Drag the centre of the bulb outwards using the tip of a small palette knife.

To garnish

Parisienne of apple lightly caramelised, or sprigs of rosemary, frosted using egg white and sugar.

A little piece of HEAVEN

A reminder of centuries past, Sign of the Angel as a historic inn is everything you'd expect: warm and cosy with large open fires, homely rooms and of course serving excellent food.

Located in the National Trust village of Lacock, Sign of the Angel is a picturesque 15th century coaching inn brought up to date by brothers Tom and Jack and their business partner and head chef Jon.

The building itself is over 500 years old and owned by the National Trust. When the lease became available two years ago, the brothers thought they'd go ahead and turn it into their own idea of a restaurant. A renovation and two AA Rosettes later and Sign of the Angel are on top form. The food offering at the inn could be described as 'modern British', but always with a unique twist and always great tasting. The menu was created with the West Country in mind: all of the produce and meat Sign of the Angel use is local and traceable, ensuring diners are only served the best. Jon might be the head chef but Tom describes the entire process as a "team effort"; all of the kitchen staff contribute to the menu, and new ideas for dishes are encouraged. The inn is actually open all day, supplying tourists and locals alike with coffee and home baked cakes in a relaxed and inviting atmosphere.

As a historic coaching inn, Sign of the Angel have five charming rooms upstairs for guests to stay in. Each cosy room is beautifully unique, decorated with antique quirks and details, but mind the beams! You'll receive a very warm welcome in your room in the form of Jon's homemade cookies, ready to settle in to your stay in Lacock. The inn also has an outside paddock area, with a beautiful garden. Throughout the summer months, guests can enjoy a cream tea by the stream.

The guys have big plans for the paddock in 2017, looking to plant and cultivate their own vegetables and herbs here to supply the kitchen. Hoping to become self-sufficient in the future, Tom and the team are also looking into farming their own pigs and sheep on the paddock.

Sign of the Angel have one goal in mind when it comes to their customers: they simply hope that each and every visitor has a memorable experience at the inn. The team are devoted to keeping standards as high as possible and pushing for improvement.

Sign of the Angel

WILD MUSHROOM, TRUFFLE & BATH SOFT CHEESE FONDANT, LEEK RISOTTO AND CONFIT ONIONS

This vegetarian main course is so simple to make but tastes so decadent.

Preparation time: 45 minutes | Cooking time: 1 hour | Serves 4

Ingredients

For the fondant:

200g wild mushrooms

100g butter

2 shallots, sliced

4 garlic cloves, chopped

5 eggs

100g plain flour

1 handful parsley, chopped

Truffle oil, to taste

40g Bath soft cheese

Salt and pepper, to taste

For the risotto:

½ leek, sliced

2 garlic cloves, finely chopped

150g Arborio rice

1 shallot

1 tbsp crème fraîche

300ml vegetable stock, warm

100ml white wine

Salt and pepper, to taste

1 tbsp rapeseed oil

For the onion:

16 silverskin onions

1 tbsp rapeseed oil

2 garlic cloves, chopped

2 tbsp red wine vinegar

1 spring thyme, chopped

For the dressing:

250g heritage tomatoes

50ml sherry vinegar

1 tsp Dijon mustard

100ml rapeseed oil

Salt and pepper, to taste

Method

For the fondant

Preheat the oven the 180°c.

Sauté the wild mushrooms, shallot and garlic in butter until browning.

Add the parsley and remove from the heat.

Blitz in a food blender and then chill.

Whisk the eggs until thick, fold in the chilled mushroom mix, and then fold in the sieved flour.

Line 4 dariole moulds with truffle oil and flour. Fill three-quarters full with mix.

Push 10g cheese into the centre of the mould and cook for 14 minutes.

For the risotto

Sauté the leeks, shallots and garlic in the rapeseed oil for a few minutes until soft, add the rice and stir for 30 seconds.

Add the white wine and reduce by half. Add half the stock and cook for a few minutes, then add the remaining stock.

Cook until rice is cooked through but still has a little 'bite' to it. Remove from the heat, and add the crème fraîche.

For the onion

Preheat the oven to 150°c.

Peel the onions and add all ingredients to an ovenproof dish and cook for 45 minutes.

Give the dish a shake halfway through cooking.

For the dressing

Blitz all the ingredients in a food processor and pass through a fine strainer.

To serve

Turn out the fondant onto a plate and serve with a portion of the risotto, topped with the confit onions.

Drizzle the dressing across the plate.

Sign of the Angel
LEMONS AND LIMES

This dish is perfect for showing off to guests, be creative with your presentation.

Preparation time: Overnight | Cooking time: 1 hour 35 minutes | Serves 6

Ingredients

For the lemon drizzle cake:

1½ large eggs

75g self-raising flour

75g caster sugar

50g granulated sugar

75g softened butter

¾ tsp baking powder

½ lemon, zest

½ lemon, juice

For the lime panna cotta:

½ lime zest

200ml milk

500ml double cream

1½ gelatine leaves

1 vanilla pod, seeds

150g caster sugar

For the lemon meringue:

½ lemon, zest

50g caster sugar

25g egg white

10g cornflour

For the lime gel:

2 limes, juice

½ tsp agar-agar powder

20g caster sugar

100ml water

For the lime yogurt:

½ lime, zest

100g natural yogurt

Method

For the lemon drizzle cake

Preheat the oven to 180°c.

In a large mixing bowl, beat together the eggs, flour, caster sugar, butter, baking powder and lemon zest until smooth. Turn into a 450g greased and lined tin.

Bake in the pre-heated oven for about 35 minutes or until golden brown in colour.

While the cake is still warm, make the lemon drizzle topping. Mix together the sugar and lemon juice and pour over the warm cake.

Leave to cool a little and loosen the sides of the cake, then lift the cake out of the tin. Cut into small portions to serve.

For the lime panna cotta

Put 6 small pudding moulds (about 120ml each) on a baking tray.

Soak the gelatine leaves in a bowl of very cold water and set aside.

Put the cream, milk and sugar into a large pan and bring slowly to the boil. When the cream is boiling, add the vanilla and stir. Then add the lime zest and whisk well. Simmer for a few minutes until reduced slightly, and then turn off the heat.

Scoop the softened gelatine out of the water and squeeze off any excess. Stir into the hot cream, leave until just warm, and then strain the cream into a jug.

Carefully pour the mix into the moulds and place in the fridge for at least 5 hours until completely set – overnight is ideal.

For the lime gel

Heat the juice, sugar and water until the sugar dissolves. Add the agar-agar powder, mix and leave to cool.

For the lemon meringue

Preheat the oven to 120°c.

Cover two baking sheets with parchment paper or foil.

Beat the egg whites until soft peaks form. Mix the flour and sugar and add very slowly, beating well between additions until the egg whites are stiff but not dry. Fold in the lemon zest.

Using a teaspoon, drop onto the baking sheet (or pipe small drops with a pastry bag).

Bake until dry but not brown for 40-45 minutes.

Cool for 2-3 minutes before removing from the baking sheets.

For the lime yoghurt

Mix the lime zest and yoghurt together, then plate.

To serve

Plate a portion of each element and dress the plate with the lime yoghurt.

Let there be MEAT

It seems like fate led to the meeting of hobby charcutiers Andy Venn and James Simpson. Two years on and Somerset Charcuterie are now an established part of the British charcuterie revolution.

Andy and James were hobby charcutiers for several years before they met. Andy grew up on a pig farm and James is a member of a small village co-operative of six families who raise livestock. They met quite by chance when their daughters became best friends at the local school and it wasn't long before they discovered that they shared a passion for curing meats and making salami.

Over a pint of cider at a local lawn-mower race – this is Somerset! – the idea for a quality British charcuterie business started to take shape. After running their own food businesses for several years, the pair were more than equipped to take on a new challenge. Within 6 months the first products were ready to try on family and friends, and with some encouraging feedback, the first farmers markets were booked. The buzz around the stall at the first market was electric and the decision was made. Somerset Charcuterie was born.

Now in their second year, the boys are going through up to a tonne of pork a week. Everything is handmade and will remain that way in order to preserve the artisan texture, flavour and look of the meat. All of the meats Andy and James produce are made following traditional Spanish, French and Italian methods, but are adapted to the British market to create a more individual product. Where possible, the boys are using other local ingredients and the cider, sage, cheese, goat, duck and wild garlic they use all come from other Somerset producers. British charcuterie is still a relatively new part of the market so quality is incredibly important. James says: "The beauty of charcuterie is that it's so versatile. You can eat it as a late supper, a light lunch or a starter. A proper board put together right looks impressive and is so tasty."

The pork Andy and James use comes from pigs that are outdoor reared. James explains: "The way a pig is bred for charcuterie is completely different to the way they are farmed for traditional meat. We work closely with our farmers to ensure standards are kept high and the product is the best it can be."

Somerset Charcuterie supplies some of the country's premium restaurants and stores and you'll also find them a little closer to home at regular farmers markets across Somerset and Bristol. They love to meet fellow meat aficionados, so pop by and say hello!

Somerset Charcuterie
THE PERFECT CHARCUTERIE BOARD

"We thought long and hard about the recipe that we should include in this book. There are hundreds of great cooking recipes that use salami, cured meats, and chorizo, but we believe the beauty of these products lies in the ease and simplicity with which you can prepare a fantastically tasty dish for sharing with friends and family."

Preparation time: 15 minutes | Serves 4-6

Ingredients

15 slices (50-60g) Somerset cider chorizo

10 slices (35-40g) black pepper and garlic salami

10 slices (35-40g) sage, mustard and cider salami

8 slices (40-50g) bresaola

10 slices (20-30g) air-dried duck breast

12 slices (60-70g) coppa

6 slices (70-90g) fully cured and dried pancetta

5 spicy chorizo pokers with cider and vintage cheddar cheese

Black olives

Pickled silverskin onions

Gherkins

Chilli peppers stuffed with cream cheese

Mixed baby leaf lettuce

1 white sourdough loaf

Method

Charcuterie boards work well as a tasty lunch, a centre piece of a buffet or prepared as a starter. Serve with some crusty bread, cheese and a glass of good wine.

Preparing a really great charcuterie board is a relatively simple thing to do; variety is the key to a board that will deliver in every sense including presentation, texture and taste.

Colours

From light pinks to rich deep reds, creamy white fat marbling, pieces of black pepper and yellow mustard seeds; ensuring that you pick a selection of meats with a variety of colours will add interest and depth to the board. Tomatoes, peppers, gherkins, onions and olives can add some brighter colours.

Textures

Try to find a selection of charcuterie products and accompaniments with an assortment of textures. For example, air dried duck or bresaola can be silky smooth. Salami sticks, with natural casings, celery sticks and gherkins can deliver a stronger bite or snap.

Flavours

There are too many diverse flavours to list here! The board opposite features pork, duck, beef, rosemary, sage, thyme, cinnamon, clove, juniper, black pepper, sea salt, garlic, mustard, paprika, chilli... The variety is endless!

Arrangement

The board – White plates, coloured plates, wooden boards, slates, marble boards; all of these can bring additional interest to your charcuterie centre piece. Our favourite is always a classic wooden board for that rustic look.

Folding – Hams, coppa, duck breast and bresaola can all be folded to give height and a natural feeling to the presentation.

Fanning – Sliced meats can be fanned on the board. Find the most attractive edge to be repeated in the fan.

Non-uniform pile – Salami or filletto can be arrange in non-uniform pile. A mix of non-uniform and uniform arrangements will prevent the board from looking too formal or too messy.

Deck of cards – Salami can also be spread like a deck of cards.

Height – A few pokers in a glass can add some height to the board.

Roll – Some of the larger slices can be rolled and laid on their long edge. Long and thin slices can be rolled and will stand up on the board.

Accompaniments

Here you can let your imagination run wild. Bread is a must and sourdough breads work especially well.

Pickles compliment the fattier meats as the vinegar cuts through and cleanses the palate.

Tomatoes, roasted peppers or stuffed red chilli peppers bring bright colours to the platter.

From Bath
WITH LOVE

A real champion of Bath's local food scene, Helen Rich and her Taste of Bath hampers aim to provide customers with the very best artisan produce that the city has to offer.

Founder and former producer herself, Helen Rich is linking customers and producers in a new and modern way. "Customers don't have time to go to every market, festival or deli, they want to find all the best produce in their area, with little or no fuss. The concept is simple; we find the best of your local artisanal produce and have it sent to your door," Helen explains.

Taste of Bath is a veritable feast of the finest artisanal produce, all sourced within a 10 mile radius of Bath. Customers can create their own hamper or select a package through Taste of Bath's beautifully designed website. Helen sends hampers all across the UK, catering for both the gifting and food tourism market.

There is a fantastic variety of produce under the Taste of Bath umbrella; from cheese and charcuterie to craft beers and gin. Each and every hamper is packed full of high quality handmade products that are truly worthy of their place. With a focus on taste and quality, Helen ensures customers can trust each product is carefully selected and the best available.

Starting in 2015 with just 13 producers, the Taste of Bath family has grown to 30 local suppliers. "It's a case of continuous discovery, I have the dream job!"

From pop up shops, markets and specialist Taste events, Bath is seeing a rise in access to local food through Taste of Bath. Helen has even taken her producers to Parliament. "The event at the palace of Westminster was great! Hobnobbing with ministers and press, some fantastic connections were made, alongside some stonking press for the producers."

Helen is a real foodie force of nature in Bath and has big plans for expanding her 'Taste of' hampers, as she hopes to bring her collective philosophy to more and more cities across the UK, starting with Oxford in early 2017.

For more information or to order your own hamper visit www.taste-of.co.uk

A Fun-Filled FARE

Legend has it that scotch eggs were invented by Fortnum and Mason in 1738 as a snack food for gentlemen travelling from Piccadilly to Bath and Bristol. Taste Fool is bringing them home again.

Head chef and chief fool Iain Kemp first began his culinary career when he was a student, working in kitchens to earn money during the holidays. After 20 years working in human resource management in London and making scotch eggs as a hobby, Iain decided to trade in his long morning commute and get back in the kitchen, investing in his hobby full time. His scotch eggs were always a big hit at family parties and it was the encouragement from his friends and family that pushed Iain to make the change.

Taste Fool creates high quality snacks that put the joy back into a packed lunch; their scotch eggs are lovingly made by hand in small batches using only the best ingredients. Customer satisfaction is the top priority for Iain and his team, and Iain believes it is their attention to detail that keeps the customers returning: "Our customers appreciate the time that goes into making the perfect scotch egg, cooking the yolk so it is just right, that sort of care makes all the difference." This kind of reliable quality comes from sourcing the finest raw ingredients available. All of the pork Taste Fool uses comes from the award-winning Larkhall Butchers and every egg is free-range and local.

Iain is often asked where he gets his inspiration for so many varieties of scotch egg, he explains: "There are so many different types of sausage so it only makes sense to try out different kinds of scotch egg." After experimenting with flavours Iain created the chorizo scotch egg, which is now a Taste Fool bestseller and this experimentation also paid off when his caramelised onion scotch egg won a Taste of the West award in 2014. Taste Fool offers a vegetarian three bean chilli egg too, but if you're looking for something with even more kick, then the hot date flavour is a must try.

Taste Fool puts the customer at the heart of everything they do and one of the best parts of Iain's job is seeing this mutual appreciation in action every Saturday at Bath Farmers Market: "The market is a hub for foodies in Bath and the atmosphere is great, interacting with customers and recognising familiar faces each week is so rewarding."

Farmhouse Cider
Scotch Egg

Chorizo
Scotch Egg

Black Pudding
Scotch Egg

COOKED PRODUCT ONLY

Taste Fool
WEST COUNTRY PLOUGHMAN'S
SCOTCH EGGS

A true local recipe, this scotch egg tastes of the West Country.

Preparation time: 30 minutes | Cooking time: 15 minutes | Serves 6

Ingredients

6 medium free-range eggs

For the sausage meat:

500g outdoor-bred pork mince

65g mature cheddar, grated

85g In a Pickle pear, apple and cider chutney or any homemade chutney

½ tsp ground coriander

¼ tsp ground ginger

½ tsp parsley

1 tsp salt

60g breadcrumbs

For the coating:

100g plain flour seasoned with a little salt and pepper

2 free-range eggs, beaten

100g breadcrumbs

Method

Boil the eggs until just soft in the middle. As a rule of thumb, 6 eggs placed into boiling water should take around 5½ minutes.

As soon as they are cooked, drain them and place them in a large bowl of ice cold water. This will stop them cooking further.

After 10 minutes, peel the eggs and refrigerate until ready to use.

To make the sausage meat, place all the ingredients in a large bowl and mix thoroughly by hand until well combined.

To 'scotch' the eggs, divide the sausage meat into 6 equally sized portions, around 110g each.

Flatten in to a burger shaped patty and then place an egg in the middle. Using wet hands carefully shape the meat around the egg, ensuring an equal layer all the way around and closing up any cracks by smoothing over with your thumb.

Continue until all the eggs are covered and place them on a baking tray lined with greaseproof paper.

To breadcrumb the eggs, arrange the flour, beaten egg and breadcrumbs in 3 separate bowls.

Dip each egg in flour. Pat to remove any excess flour and then dip into the beaten egg until covered.

Roll in the breadcrumbs and gently press between the hands to ensure they stick.

Place back on the tray and continue until all the eggs are coated.

Preheat oven to 190°c.

Fry the eggs at 170°c in a deep fat fryer for 2 minutes.

Once cooked, remove them from the fryer and place on a baking tray lined with clean greaseproof paper.

Bake in the oven for 7 minutes.

Woven
IN TIME

Housed in a 17ᵗʰ century textiles mill, The Weaving Shed
has the best views in Bradford on Avon.

Having previously worked under Michelin-starred chefs such as Michael Caines and Gordon Ramsay, head chef and owner of The Weaving Shed Richard Synan knows all about top quality food. Situated right by the side of the River Avon, diners are treated to a magnificent view across the river while they eat, through The Weaving Shed's floor to ceiling windows.

Front of house duties are handled by the experienced hand of Richard's wife, Natasha, who's impressive career includes Lewtrenchard Manor, Gidleigh Park and the Old Bell Hotel in Malmesbury.

The restaurant itself is entirely open plan, including the kitchen. If you have a question for the chefs, don't be shy! The Weaving Shed is a place for people to relax, unwind and enjoy good food and the welcoming atmosphere is what sets the restaurant apart. Richard truly believes that great food should not be expensive and The Weaving Shed embodies this ethos: high quality food at a competitive price. In the kitchen, Richard employs passionate, like-minded chefs, not cooks. This is why everything the kitchen serves is 100 percent made on site by his team, including all their sauces and chutneys.

The Weaving Shed is open all day from 10am, serving everything from homemade cakes and pastries to light lunches and fantastic brunches at the weekend. Dinner is the main event; this is where the chefs have the chance to show off their skills. Cooking up modern British food, the menu is designed to appeal to every type of diner.

The Weaving Shed take their drinks seriously, with an extensive wine list and a wide range of premium lagers and craft beers on offer. The bar also serves cocktails and has a dedicated gin and tonic menu. From old favourites to in-house inventions, you're sure to find a suitable thirst-quencher on the menu. Don't worry, all of their cocktails are made using premium spirits and mixers, only the best will do.

Excellent food starts with excellent produce and The Weaving Shed is ideally situated to take advantage of what the south west has to offer, but Richard isn't afraid of searching further afield to find exactly what he's looking for. Flying Fish in Cornwall supply the restaurant with fresh fish and their mushrooms come from Wiltshire-based Marlborough Mushrooms. For a delicious meal accompanied by stunning views, be sure to visit The Weaving Shed.

The Weaving Shed
PAN FRIED SEA BREAM, GNOCCHI, SHELLFISH VELOUTÉ

Why buy ready-made gnocchi from the supermarket when it's so easy to make yourself at home? Paired with sea bream it makes a beautifully light summer dish.

Preparation time: 30 minutes | Cooking time: 10 minutes | Serves 4

Ingredients

4 fillet sea bream

8 tiger prawns

100g samphire

Olive oil for frying

For the gnocchi:

250g potato

67g type 00 pasta flour

½ egg, beaten

Salt

For the shellfish velouté:

1 shallot, sliced

250ml white wine

250ml vermouth

500ml shellfish stock

500ml cream

Lemon juice to season

Method

For the gnocchi

Place the potatoes in a pan with water and bring to the boil. Boil for 15 minutes until they are soft enough to cut with a knife. Drain the potatoes and mash them.

Make the gnocchi by combining all of the ingredients together in a bowl and mix to form a ball.

Turn out onto a lightly floured work surface and knead for 5 minutes.

Cut into desired shape, usually small ovals, and drop into salted boiling water until they float.

For the sauce

To make the sauce, put the shallots, white wine and vermouth into a pan and simmer until the liquid has evaporated.

Add the shellfish stock, bring to the boil and reduce by half. Add the cream and bring to the boil. Season with salt and a little lemon juice.

For the fish

Fry the fish in a non-stick pan with a little oil and the tiger prawns. Cook the bream skin-side down for 2 minutes, or until the skin is crispy. Turn the fish to cook on the other side.

Just before serving, add the samphire to the pan to warm it through.

To serve

Place the gnocchi on the plate first and place the fish on top.

Spoon over the prawns and samphire, then pour over the sauce and serve.

The Weaving Shed

STICKY TOFFEE PUDDING, PECAN CRUNCH, VANILLA ICE-CREAM AND TOFFEE SAUCE

Sticky toffee pudding is a classic crowd-pleasing dessert. The addition here of the pecan crunch topping makes it just that bit more decadent.

Preparation time: 20 minutes | Cooking time: 1 hour | Serves 4

Ingredients

For the sticky toffee pudding:

120g unsalted butter

185g soft dark brown sugar

4 eggs

225g self-raising flour

2 tbsp instant coffee

225g chopped dates

300ml boiling water

1 tbsp bicarbonate of soda

400g good quality vanilla ice cream

For the pecan crunch:

30g pecans

30g soft dark brown sugar

30g butter

30g plain flour

12g maple syrup

For the toffee sauce:

100g butter

100g soft dark brown sugar

100g golden syrup

400g cream

Method

For the sticky toffee pudding

Preheat the oven to 180°c.

Combine the dates, coffee, bicarbonate of soda and boiling water in a bowl and leave to cool completely.

Beat the butter and sugar in a stand mixer until light and fluffy. Slowly add the eggs one by one ensuring that they are fully incorporated after each addition.

Once added, slowly add the flour a spoonful at a time. Then add the date mixture and mix completely.

Pour the mix into individual dishes and bake in the oven for 25 minutes, until a knife inserted comes out clean.

For the pecan crunch

Combine all the ingredients in a bowl and rub between your fingers until the butter has softened and combined with the rest of the ingredients.

Spread onto a tray and bake in the oven at 180°c for 15 minutes.

Allow to cool and break up with a rolling pin – this is the fun part!

For the sauce

Put the butter, sugar and syrup in a pan and bring to the boil.

Once boiled, add the cream and bring back to the boil.

To serve

Sprinkle the pecan crunch on top of the cooked sticky toffee pudding and serve with a big spoon of vanilla ice cream and the toffee sauce poured on top.

Setting
THE BAR

In keeping with tradition, The Wheatsheaf Combe Hay is a family-run country inn. The Barton family have been residents of the Domesday village of Combe Hay for about 25 years and took over The Wheatsheaf Inn ten years ago.

The Barton family consists of Ian and Adele Barton, their son James who is the manager and faithful hounds Margaux and Gloria - working cocker spaniels who's most important role is meeting and greeting guests and generally spreading goodwill. The dogs are named after two significant Bordeaux chateaux - reflecting Ian and James' love of fine European wine. This is also evident in the very fine wine list and exclusive wines available to diners at The Wheatsheaf. James offers a bespoke wine service too, providing clients with collections of fine wine for their personal cellars at home.

James and Ian prefer to start trends rather than follow the pack when it comes to their drinks: they are always on the lookout for new and different beers and lagers whilst still providing customers with a selection of traditional real ales. The Wheatsheaf is lucky enough to be based less than a mile away from cider maker Honey and Daughter, whose ciders they regularly stock. It doesn't really get much more local than that!

Alongside great drinks comes great food. With long-standing head chef Eddy Rains at the helm in the kitchen, The Wheatsheaf has an enviable reputation for superb food which is strictly local and purely seasonal. Happy hens provide delicious fresh eggs for breakfasts and the busy Wheatsheaf bees supply the inn with home-grown honey. Everything is homemade on the premises by Eddy's capable team in the kitchen, from the freshly baked bread to the tempting petit fours. Ian is a countryman at heart and throughout the season he provides plenty of partridge, pheasant and game for the menu as well as rod-caught fish. The team are serious about food! The Wheatsheaf also has a small vegetable garden that subsidises the kitchen, ensuring 100 percent freshness on all the produce they plate up.

Although just a short drive from the centre of Bath, The Wheatsheaf is a world away from the hustle and bustle of the city. Arriving at the inn, you turn a corner into stunning countryside; truly rural bliss. This is why many choose to stay in the understated but luxurious rooms at The Wheatsheaf, which are located in a separate building in the garden. Perfect for a peaceful break!

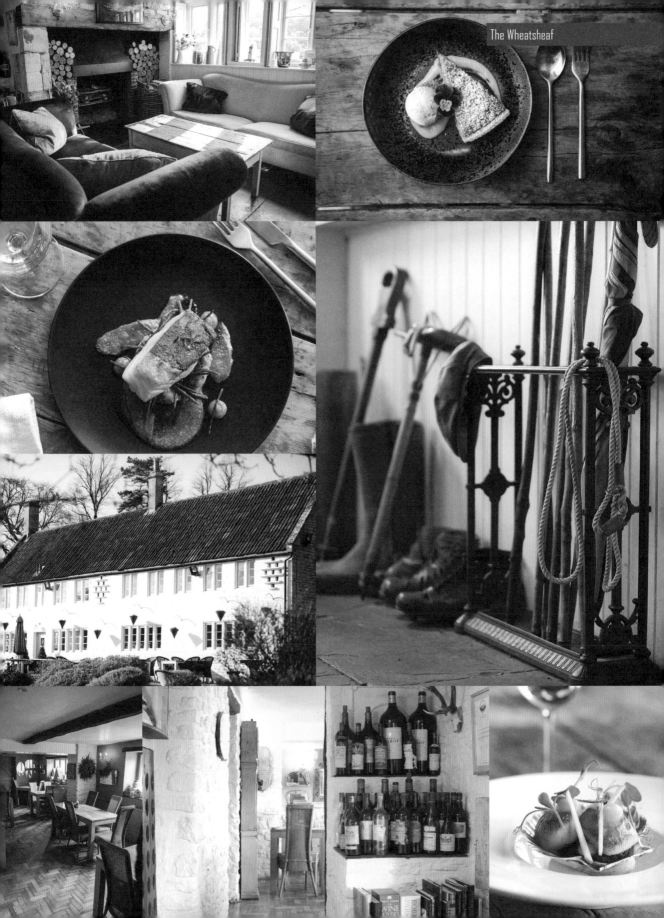

The Wheatsheaf

The Wheatsheaf
ASHCOMBE ESTATE PARTRIDGE KIEV, BEETROOT FIVE WAYS

The partridge here makes a great alternative to chicken; a really rather rich starter.

Preparation time: 30 minutes | Cooking time: 45 minutes | Serves 4 as a starter

Ingredients

For the Kiev:

2 partridge crowns

200g unsalted butter

2 garlic cloves

1 handful flat leaf parsley, chopped

Maldon salt and freshly ground black pepper

200g plain flour

2 eggs

Panko breadcrumbs

For the beetroot ketchup:

4 large beetroot

200ml white wine vinegar

200g caster sugar

A splash red wine

For the beetroot pickle:

6 baby beetroot, peeled

200ml white wine vinegar

100g caster sugar

1 star anise

4 black peppercorns

For the beetroot crisps:

4 striped beetroot, sliced

Rapeseed oil

Sea salt, to taste

For the salt baked beetroot:

1 large beetroot

2 egg whites

100g table salt

For the beetroot slaw:

1 large beetroot, grated

1 carrot, peeled and grated

1 small bunch dill, chopped

1 banana shallot, finely sliced

Rapeseed oil

Method

For the Kiev

For the Kiev, remove the breast from the crown with a boning knife. Remove the skin and trim off any sinew.

Cover with cling film and lightly beat the breasts to tenderise the meat.

Crush the garlic and combine with the butter, salt and pepper and chopped parsley to make the garlic butter.

Pipe the butter down the middle of the breast and wrap the breast into a sausage using cling film to encase the butter.

Chill until the butter hardens, then coat in flour, egg then breadcrumbs. Dip back into the egg then breadcrumbs again to double coat the Kiev, this prevents any of the butter from seeping out.

To cook

Cook the Kiev for 1 minute in a deep fat fryer at 180°c, then 5 minutes in an oven at 180°c. Rest the Kiev for 1 minute while plating the garnish.

For the beetroot ketchup

For the ketchup, boil the beetroot in salted water until soft to the knife. Peel the skin, then roughly chop. Add to a pan with sugar, vinegar and red wine. Boil until the liquid has reduced by half. Blitz the beetroot in a liquidiser adding the liquid bit by bit to obtain the correct consistency.

For the pickle

Peel the beetroot and blanch in salted boiling water. Bring the other ingredients up to the boil and submerge the cooked beetroot. Leave to cool and pickle.

For the crisps

Preheat the oven to 80°c. Slice the beetroot on a mandoline or using a sharp knife. Add a little rapeseed oil and sea salt and crisp in the oven on a tray.

For the salt baked beetroot

Preheat the oven to 180°c. Make a paste with the egg white and salt. Cover the beetroot and bake for 30-45 minutes or until the beetroot is soft to the knife. Peel the crust and skin and dice the beetroot.

For the slaw

Combine the grated beetroot, carrot and sliced shallot with the rapeseed oil, chopped dill, salt and pepper.

Woods
OVEN ROASTED GROUSE WITH ROOT VEGETABLES AND THYME

Woods opened in 1979, with owners David and Claude Price offering an upmarket but informal restaurant environment, serving affordable food to match. Now, 37 years later, children of regulars from the early days bring their own children along to show them where mummy and daddy experienced their first taste of food with a French accent. This is a true family business, with head chef Stuart Ash having being in charge of the kitchen for the past 23 years. He has been helped for the past 13 years by Joe, David and Claude's son-in-law, and Gaston their son, who did all his training under the watchful eye of Stuart. Woods takes a refreshingly uncomplicated approach to the menu: all dishes are cooked to order with a French ethos. "Change may give us new branches to explore, but continuity gives us roots."

Preparation time: 20 minutes | Cooking time: 30 minutes | Serves 4

Ingredients

4 grouse, plucked and prepared

1 carrot, peeled and diced

1 parsnip, peeled and diced

1 small swede, peeled and diced

1 small bunch of thyme

Salt and pepper, to season

Sunflower oil, for cooking

For the sauce:

285ml red wine

285 ml veal stock

For the game chips:

Vegetable oil, for deep-frying

1 large baking potato, sliced very thinly on a mandoline

Salt and pepper, to season

Method

For the vegetables

Preheat an oven to 200°c. Put the diced vegetables in an oven tray with sunflower oil and seasoning, cover with tin foil and place in a hot oven to cook for 15 minutes.

When the vegetables are just cooked remove the tin foil and continue to cook for 5 minutes, occasionally mixing. When cooked, drain them well.

For the sauce

Put all of the red wine in a pan on the hob and reduce by half. Add the veal stock and reduce again by half. Once reduced, keep to one side.

For the game chips

Heat the vegetable oil in a deep, heavy-bottomed saucepan until a small cube of bread sizzles and turns golden-brown when dropped into it.

Deep-fry the potato slices for 1-2 minutes, or until crisp and golden brown. Remove the game chips from the oil with a slotted spoon and set aside to drain on kitchen paper. Season with the salt and pepper.

For the grouse

Preheat the oven to 200°c. Season the grouse with salt and pepper. Pan-fry the grouse until it is light brown all over and then cook in a hot oven for approximately 7-9 minutes.

When the birds are just cooked, leaving the meat pink, remove from the oven and rest for 5 minutes.

To serve

Heat the sauce and re-heat the vegetables. Sauce the plate and add a spoonful of vegetables on each.

Place the grouse on top of the vegetables and garnish with the game chips and a sprig of thyme.

Woods

Weird and Wonderful WINES

Hungary. Japan. India. Wales. These are just some of the places Ben Franks and Gyorgy Zsiga source their wines from. Specialising in the "undiscovered" and "unexpected" wines from across the world, the aim of their new venture Novel Wines is simply to impart this love onto everyone else.

Ben and Gyorgy love wine. Working previously as a freelance journalist writing about wine and a wine consultant, there's not much Ben doesn't know about the drink. Together with his partner, Hungarian wine importer Gyorgy, they are bringing a whole host of more interesting wines to the UK market.

After their success holding tasting events of these unusual wines, the decision to establish Novel Wines as an online retailer seemed the next logical step to Ben and Gyorgy, as Ben explains: "There was so much excitement surrounding the product and the feedback was great, we knew there needed to be somewhere people could purchase the wine."

With the start-up costs for Novel Wines raised by a Crowdfunder project in just 28 days, Ben has his sights set firmly on the future, hoping to open a bricks and mortar tasting bar in Bath, serving small plates with each wine.

Ben describes the Novel Wines stock selection as "weird and wonderful"; it all comes from unusual places that are not famed for their vineyards. Of course, there are tons of retailers out there offering exclusive wines. What makes Novel Wines unique is the passion that goes into selecting each bottle. Every single wine that Ben and Gyorgy stock is personally hand-picked and rigorously taste-tested, which means each wine is of the very best quality. Average is not good enough; Novel Wines aim to surprise and excite their drinker with every bottle. Ben elaborates: "You can only really get someone to try a weird wine once so it needs to delight them from the very first taste."

While Novel Wines stocks bottles from across the world, their main selection comes from England, Wales and Hungary, the pair's specialist areas. In particular, there is a selection from Somerset itself, including a dry white wine from the Oatley Vineyard. If you'd prefer a rosé, try the bottle by Dunleavy's, based just outside of Bristol. Novel Wines are also supporting social enterprise wine merchant Vin2o, which sources its wines from Bordeaux. Vin2o puts clean water projects first, donating 100% of their profits to Bristol-based charity Frank Water.

Wine MATCHING

Ben and Gyorgy at Novel Wines have recommended wines that pair perfectly with all the delicious dishes in this book. Every bottle is available to buy now at novelwines.co.uk.

BATH CAKE COMPANY

Maple and Pecan Chocolate Drip Cake

Monsoon Valley Late Harvest Chenin Blanc 2015, THAILAND, £12.50

This gloriously indulgent cake from our friends at the Bath Cake Co would be ideal with the crushed red-apple sticky sweet Chenin Blanc. The wine's honey and quince notes also go very well with pecan nuts and pretzels!

THE BATH PUB COMPANY

THE CHEQUERS

Hay ash venison with red cabbage, pickled brambles and hazelnut gnocchi

Babylonstoren Babel 2014, SOUTH AFRICA, £12.90

A gorgeously fruity Bordeaux blend with a dollop of Shiraz, ripe and gutsy but not overbearing so it's ideal with a venison dish like this.

THE HARE AND HOUNDS

Roast cod fillet with chorizo and butter bean cassoulet with lemon, garlic and parsley dressing

Kyperounda Petritis 2015, CYPRUS, £13.50

Rich and fresh roast white cod, lemon and garlic match with Kyperounda's mouth-watering acidity. Citrus, vanilla and candied lime notes in the wine play off the chorizo and butterbean elements well.

THE MARLBOROUGH TAVERN

Pan-fried brill, parmentier potatoes, cauliflower two ways and pickled fennel

Grace Koshu Kayagatake 2015, JAPAN, £17.90

This wonderful, classic white fish dish works brilliantly with our elegant white from Yamanashi Provence in Japan. This citrus, clean white wine has notes not too dissimilar from sake and a finish that truly endures. Delightful!

THE LOCKSBROOK INN

Banoffee

Round Hill Roastery Kanganu AB Espresso,
KENYA, £7.00 (250g)

This espresso from Round Hill Roastery would be fab with this deconstructed banoffee. The smooth coffee has notes of cranberry, prune and marzipan.

THE BEAUFORT

Grilled Cornish monkfish and octopus yellow curry with coconut rice and Asian slaw

Sula Vineyard Dindori Reserve Viognier 2015,
INDIA, £10.90

A top class pairing with an exotic curry like this is a bottle of Sula's Viognier. Distinctive, fresh and tropical notes, slight vanilla sweetness, and a full bodied mouthfeel tell us that it's born to go with a great curry!

THE BUNCH OF GRAPES

Soy cured salmon in a cucumber cup with mango salsa and wasabi crème fraîche

Ancre Hill Estate Blanc de Blancs 2009, WALES, £32.90

Try a bottle of this creamy, mature sparkling Chardonnay with elements of conference pears, vanilla and buttered honey. It's a stylish Welsh bubbly to pair with an equally stylish canapé!

FAT FOWL

Pan fried hake fillet with crab and chorizo risotto and salsa verde

Hubertus Clusserath Trittenheimer Apotheke Riesling
Spatlese 2011, GERMANY, £13.50

Risotto and beautiful quality Riesling like this one from the Mosel Valley are matches to be savoured. The racy, mineral elements pair with the seafood while its sweetness contrasts the risotto and stands up to the salsa verde and chorizo.

THE GEORGE

Pan fried venison with a Hunter's Pie on a bed of savoy cabbage and bacon

Tibor Gal Titi Bikaver 2013, HUNGARY, £12.90

This spicy Hungarian red blend from Eger in the north of the country is full of cherry and forest fruits. It's a lovely complement to something like venison, while having enough body to stand up to the pie and bacon elements well.

THE GREENHOUSE

Mackerel brandade

Wraxall Bacchus 2015, ENGLAND, £12.90

This aromatic and zippy white wine from Somerset is crying out for the smokiness of the mackerel, adding freshness and class. Delightful!

HARTLEY FARM

Chilli, lime and coriander spatchcock chicken, jalapeño cornbread, with an avocado and tomato salsa

Sula Vineyards Dindori Reserve Shiraz 2015, INDIA, £12.50

This surprisingly delicious Shiraz from Maharashtra, India, is smoky and bursting with blackberries, blueberries and vanilla. It partners with spice and tomato superbly well!

IN A PICKLE

St Stephen's Pie

Borovitza Bella Rada 2015, BULGARIA, £15.50

We think you'd struggle to find a finer match than the beautifully creamy, mature Bella Rada than with this household favourite pie. The Bella has glimpses of tropical fruit, nutmeg and peppery spice, perfect with buttery pastry and white sauce.

JAMIE'S FARM

Puff pastry pie with aubergine, tomato and mozzarella

Vina Koslovic Teran 2014, CROATIA, £11.90

A fresh and medium-bodied red from Croatia's most famous region. Its Mediterranean-influence red berry fruit is a fab match with the veg and cheese, while the wine's oak influence will match that buttery pastry like peas in a pod.

LARKHALL BUTCHERS

Steak tartare gratin, from Ma Cuisine

Gaia Notios Agiorgitiko/Syrah 2015, GREECE, £11.90

Velvety and intense red wine with Mediterranean aromas of juicy red berries – and my golly this wine's smooth! It's a charm alongside steak tartare.

MES AMIS

Three cheese muffins with pea, sweet chilli and mint dip

Chateau Ksara Blanc de Blancs 2015, LEBANON, £12.90

Alongside Mes Amis' spin on cheese muffins, we think this ultra-weird n' wonderful bottle of Lebanese white will go beautifully. Aromas of hazelnut and exotic fruits give way to spice, pineapple, vanilla and nuts on the palate.

THE METHUEN ARMS

Chargrilled lamb rump with stuffed tomato, borlotti beans, onion squash, green olives

Kayra Okuzgozu 2013, TURKEY, £14.90

Wow, this is an undiscovered gem of Turkey. Subtle tannins, cherry, leather, herbs and delicate spices make it our favourite choice with something like chargrilled lamb. Give it a try!

THE REDAN INN

Raw and pickled beetroot, truffled goat's cheese, hay ash

Figula Olaszrizling 2015, HUNGARY, £9.90

This is a juicy, mouth-watering white wine with green herbs, wet stone and lemon. A vibrant wine like this needs pickled beetroot's sweetness and the creaminess of the goat's cheese. Lovely match!

THE RIVER HOUSE

Crab toast with herb aioli

Oatley Jane's Madeleine Angevine 2014, ENGLAND, £13.50

Fresh crab deserves the elegance of a wine like Oatley Jane's. Full of aromas of English blossom and elderflower pressé, it's a fine match with the herb aioli.

THE ROYAL CRESCENT HOTEL

Hay Smoked Salmon, cauliflower, radish and lemon

Ancre Hill Estate Chardonnay 2014, WALES, £24.90

This buttery, full bodied Welsh white wine will match delightfully well with the oily texture and smokiness of the salmon. The wine has a zippy, long finish, perfect with food!

SEVEN STARS

Fillet of beef with beetroot purée, dauphinoise potatoes and a red wine and Port reduction

Stobi Signature Vranec Veratis Reserve 2013, MACEDONIA, £14.90

Deep plum coloured red wines like this were made for beef. Notes of chocolate, cherry and coffee give the wine a full body that charms the socks off a meat even as high quality as a fillet like this. Heaven!

SIGN OF THE ANGEL

Wild mushroom, truffle and Bath Soft Cheese fondant, leek risotto, confit onions with tomato dressing

Zsirai Sisters Furmint 2013, HUNGARY, £12.50

Making the best of Tokaj's flagship grape, Furmint, the Zsirai sisters have made a full and rounded white wine with rich baked apple, buttery oak and beautiful minerality. It's gorgeous with buttery, mushroom-based risottos.

Lemons and Limes

Camel Valley "Cornwall" Brut 2013, ENGLAND, £28.90

While many people might rush for the dessert wine to match, we reckon a bottle of Camel Valley's leading bubbly will work even better. A fine, traditional method fizz that's mouth-watering alongside the citrus in this dessert.

THE SHRUBBERY

Iced Apple Parfait with Calvados

Kardos Tundermese "Fairytale" 2015, HUNGARY, £13.50

This is simply everyone's favourite dessert wine… Fresh acidity, honey, melon, quince and pear flavours will play off the apple in this dish perfectly!

SOMERSET CHARCUTERIE

The Perfect Charcuterie Board

Monsoon Valley Red 2015, THAILAND, £9.90

A fantastic charcuterie board like this goes stunningly well with a soft, rounded red. Our very novel red blend from Monsoon Valley in Thailand is layered with plums, leather and a gentle sweetness perfect with chorizo and salami.

TASTE FOOL

West Country Ploughman's scotch eggs

Oatley Leonora's 2014, ENGLAND, £13.50

Sticking to the West Country, try this refreshing and crisp aromatic white from south Somerset. It cuts through the fat of a scotch egg and makes for the perfect picnic wine!

THE WEAVING SHED

Pan fried sea bream, gnocchi, shellfish velouté

Prima Donna Sauvignon Blanc 2015, URUGUAY, £19.90

We think this full bodied, tropical and incredibly mouth-watering Sauvignon Blanc from the southern hemisphere is the only thing that can do this fresh sea bream dish justice. Pure summer luxury.

Sticky toffee pudding, pecan crunch, vanilla ice cream and toffee sauce

Denbies Noble Harvest 2015, ENGLAND, £23.90

Our premium, utterly gorgeous dessert wine from Surrey – the Noble Harvest – is an indulgence of honey and citrus, delicious with the nuts, cream and toffee of this dessert.

THE WHEATSHEAF

Ashcombe Estate partridge Kiev, beetroot five ways

Takler Kékfrankos Reserve 2013, HUNGARY, £19.90

To match gamey partridge and the sweet freshness of the beetroot one might immediately think of Pinot Noir. Instead, why not treat yourself to this gorgeous Kékfrankos with fine cherry notes and a smooth, remarkably long finish.

WOODS

Oven roasted grouse with root vegetables and thyme

Babylonstoren Farm "Limited Edition" Nebukadnesar 2013, SOUTH AFRICA, £28.90

Worldwide exclusive to Novel Wines, the 'Neb' is a mind-blowingly good wine. Modelled on the great grapes of Bordeaux but with its own distinctive character, this wine is something special and beautiful with root veg and oven-roasted meats.

The DIRECTORY

These great local businesses have supported the making of this book; please support and enjoy them.

Bath Cake Company
14 Fountain Buildings
Lansdown Mews
Bath
BA1 5DX
Tel: 01225 446094
Web: www.bathcakecompany.co.uk
Bespoke celebration and wedding cake maker and decorating school based in the heart of Bath.

The Bath Gin Company
2/3 Queen Street
Bath
BA1 1HE
Tel: 01225 462457
Web: www.thebathgincompany.co.uk
The Canary Gin Bar is dedicated to all things Bath Gin; serving perfect gin and tonics and expertly mixed gin cocktails.

Bath College
The Shrubbery
Avon Street
Bath
BA1 1UP
Tel: 01225 328502
Web: www.bathcollege.ac.uk
A restaurant offering formal and modern dining for lunch and dinner, all of the dishes are prepared, served and cooked by students at Bath College.

The Bath Pub Company

The Chequers
50 Rivers Street
Bath
BA1 2QA
Tel: 01225 360017
Web: www.thechequersbath.com

The Hare and Hounds
Lansdown Road
Bath
BA1 5TJ
Tel: 01225 482682
Web: www.hareandhoundsbath.com

The Locksbrook Inn
103 Locksbrook Road
Bath
BA1 3EN
Tel: 01225 427119
Web: www.thelocksbrookinn.com

The Marlborough Tavern
35 Marlborough Buildings
Bath
BA1 2LY
Tel: 01225 423731
Web: www.marlborough-tavern.com
Modern gastropubs, located across Bath city centre, each individual in style, serving restaurant quality food in a relaxed setting.

The Beaufort
1, Beaufort
London Road
Bath
BA1 6QB
Tel: 01225 422033
Web: www.thebeaufortbath.com
A family run restaurant in the heart of Larkhall serving high quality, creative, seasonal food.

Beth's Bakes
Beth Al Rikabi
www.bethsbakes.com
beth@bethsbakes.com
Tel: 07507 571300
Twitter: @bethsbakes
Instagram: beththefreerangechef
Facebook: Beth The Free-range Chef
Chef for hire, cooking her way across the world. Find her at pop-ups and supper clubs in the west country.

The Bunch of Grapes
14 Silver Street
Bradford on Avon
BA15 1JY
Tel: 01225 938088
Web: www.thebunchofgrapes.com
Inspired by the village bar bistros of south west France, the Bunch of Grapes is open for lunch and dinner every day. Serving classic French dishes alongside an extensive hand-picked wine list.

Fat Fowl

Silver Street
Bradford on Avon
Wiltshire
BA15 1JX
Tel: 01225 863111
Web: www.fatfowl.com

The Fat Fowl Restaurant is situated in the centre of Bradford on Avon just outside Bath. It is a bustling licensed cafe by day, a quality restaurant in the evening, and everything in between.

The George

67 Woolley Street
Bradford on Avon
BA15 1AQ
Tel: 01225 865650
Web: thegeorgebradfordonavon.co.uk

A quirky country inn serving hearty pub grub, inspired by the seasons and sourced from the surrounding countryside.

The Greenhouse Restaurant

The Pavilion
Wadswick Green
Corsham
SN13 9RD
Tel: 01225 585880
Web: www.thegreenhousewg.co.uk

The Greenhouse is a smart, stylish and relaxed new dining destination built on the old derelict Royal Arthur Park site at Wadswick Green.

Hartley Farm Shop and Kitchen

Winsley
Bradford on Avon
Wiltshire
BA15 2JB
Tel: 01225 864948
Web: www.hartley-farm.co.uk

Neston Farm Shop and Kitchen

Atworth
Wiltshire
SN12 8HP
Tel: 01225 700881
www.nestonfarmshop.co.uk

Family-run farm shops and cafés dedicated to producing and serving excellent food, with a focus on provenance and quality.

Honey and Daughter Cider

Upper Midford Farm
Midford
Bath
BA2 7EJ
Web: www.honeyanddaughter.co.uk

A family run business making scrumptious, full-bodied craft cider using classic Somerset apple varieties and traditional techniques.

In A Pickle

Tel: 01225 72255
Web: www.inapicklefoodco.co.uk

Handmade artisan pickles and chutneys, created using the freshest ingredients.

Jamie's Farm

Hill House Farm
Ditteridge
Box
Wiltshire
SN13 8QA

Jamie's Farm is a children's charity transforming the lives of vulnerable children in challenging urban schools. Providing a unique combination of 'farming, family and therapy' through a short stay residential and follow up programme.

Kettlesmith Brewery

Unit 16
Treenwood Industrial Estate
Bradford on Avon
Wiltshire
BA15 2AU
Tel: 01225 864839
Web: www.kettlesmithbrewing.com

Kettlesmith Brewing Co. is a craft brewery making modern and accessible beers that complement any menu and taste.

Larkhall Butchers

1 Lambridge Buildings
Larkhall
Bath
BA1 6RS
Tel: 01225 313987
Web: www.larkhallbutchers.co.uk

Situated in the heart of Larkhall village just outside of Bath city centre, Larkhall Butchers artfully combines the counter service of a traditional butchery with the professionalism of people passionate about food.

Mes Amis

12 Bath Road
Beckington
Frome
BA11 6SW
Tel: 01373 830723

Bustling local deli, café and village store based in Beckington serving everything from tempting tarts and frittatas to focaccia and salads.

The Methuen Arms

2 High Street
Corsham
Wiltshire
SN13 0HB
Tel: 01249 717060
Web: www.themethuenarms.com

The Methuen Arms is an award-winning Great British inn, where hospitality meets fabulous food and drink in a comfortable setting.

New Macdonalds Farm

Closes Farm
Kingsdown
Corsham
Wiltshire
SN13 8DG
Tel: 01225 519820
Twitter: @MatthewAndLou

A high welfare farm located on the outskirts of Bath, specialising in outdoor reared rare-breed meat and eggs.

Novel Wines
11 Manvers Street
Bath
BA1 1JQ
Tel: 01225 519820
Web: www.novelwines.co.uk
An independent online wine merchant specialising in undiscovered wines from all over the world.

The Redan Inn
Fry's Well
Chilcompton
Radstock
Somerset
BA3 4HA
Tel: 01761 258560
Web: www.theredaninn.co.uk
The Redan Inn is a newly refurbished public house with seven boutique rooms and an excellent restaurant.

The River House
7 The Bridge
Frome
Somerset
BA11 1AR
Tel: 01373 464847
Web: www.riverhousefrome.co.uk
Café-bar open all day for fabulous coffee and home-cooked food. Head here in the evening for a cocktail or two!

The Royal Crescent Hotel and Spa
16 Royal Crescent
Bath
BA1 2LS
Tel: 01225 823333
Web: www.royalcrescent.co.uk
Overlooking the secluded gardens of The Royal Crescent Hotel and Spa, the AA 3 Rosette Dower House Restaurant remains one of Bath's best-kept secrets, offering award winning dining throughout the year to hotel guests and non-residents.

The Seven Stars
Winsley
Bradford on Avon
Wiltshire
BA15 2LQ
Tel: 01225 722204
Web: www.sevenstarswinsley.co.uk
Friendly country inn serving uncomplicated, great tasting food.

Sign of the Angel
6 Church Street
Lacock
Wiltshire
SN15 2LB
Tel: 01249 730230
Web: www.signoftheangel.co.uk
A two AA Rosette awarded 15th century coaching inn with a restaurant and rooms, located in the National Trust village of Lacock.

Somerset Charcuterie
Lowerstock Farm
Bakers Lane
Wrington
BS40 5HT
Tel: 07866 636463
Web: www.somersetcharcuterie.com
Artisan charcutiers based in Wiltshire. Find them at various food festivals across the UK.

Taste Fool
Woodland View
Devizes Road
Box
SN13 8EB
Tel: 01249 715547
Web: www.tastefool.co.uk
Facebook: facebook.com/thetastefool
Twitter: @thetastefool
From handmade scotch eggs to pork pies and hummus, Taste Fool create lots of lovely things for on-the-go lunches or picnics.

Taste of Bath
Tel: 01225 683021
Web: www.taste-of.co.uk
Taste of Bath hampers specialise in hyper local artisan food, sourced within a ten-mile radius of the city of Bath.

Visit Bath
Abbey Churchyard
Bath
BA1 1LY
Tel: 01225 322428
Web: www.visitbath.co.uk
Bath's official visitor information service.

The Weaving Shed
3 Bridge Yard
Kingston Mills
Bradford on Avon
Wiltshire
BA15 1EJ
Tel: 01225 866519
Web: www.weaving-shed.co.uk
Located right next to the River Avon in Bradford on Avon, The Weaving Shed cooks up Great British food with stunning views.

The Wheatsheaf
Combe Hay
Bath
BA2 7EG
Tel: 01225 833504
Web: www.wheatsheafcombehay.com
The Wheatsheaf Combe Hay is a country pub in the time honoured tradition - a place to eat, drink and sleep. Serving top quality seasonal food alongside the finest wine and beer list.

Woods
9 -13 Alfred Street
Bath
BA1 2QX
Tel: 01225 314812
Web: www.woodsrestaurant.com
The family-run Woods occupies the ground floor of five Georgian town houses in a quiet cul de sac opposite the Assembly Rooms. With its Georgian elegance and warm informal atmosphere Woods has created an enviable reputation in Bath.

Other titles in the 'Get Stuck In' series

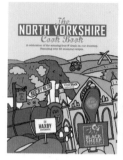

The North Yorkshire Cook Book
features Andrew Pern, Visit
York, Made in Malton, Black
Sheep Brewery and lots more.
978-1-910863-12-1

The Birmingham Cook Book
features Glynn Purnell, The
Smoke Haus, Loaf Bakery,
Simpsons and lots more.
978-1-910863-10-7

The Bristol Cook Book
features Dean Edwards, Lido,
Clifton Sausage, The Ox, and
wines from Corks of Cotham
plus lots more.
978-1-910863-14-5

The Oxfordshire Cook Book
features Mike North of The
Nut Tree Inn, Sudbury House,
Jacobs Inn, The Muddy Duck
and lots more.
978-1-910863-08-4

The Lancashire Cook Book
features Andrew Nutter of
Nutters Restaurant, Bertram's,
The Blue Mallard and lots
more.
978-1-910863-09-1

The Liverpool Cook Book
features Burnt Truffle, The
Art School, Fraiche, Villaggio
Cucina and many more.
978-1-910863-15-2

**The Sheffield Cook Book
- Second Helpings**
features Jameson's Tea Rooms,
Craft & Dough, The Wortley
Arms, The Holt, Grind Café
and lots more.
978-1-910863-16-9

The Derbyshire Cook Book
features Chatsworth
Estate, Fischer's of Baslow,
Thornbridge Brewery and lots
more.
978-0-9928981-7-5

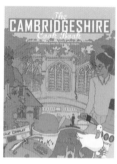

The Cambridgeshire Cook Book
features Daniel Clifford of
Midsummer House, The Pint
Shop, Gog Magog Hills, Clare
College and lots more.
978-0-9928981-9-9

The Suffolk Cook Book
features Jimmy Doherty of
Jimmy's Farm, Gressingham
Duck and lots more.
978-1-910863-02-2

The Manchester Cook Book
features Aiden Byrne, Simon
Rogan, Harvey Nichols and
lots more.
978-1-910863-01-5

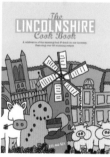

The Lincolnshire Cook Book
features Colin McGurran of
Winteringham Fields,
TV chef Rachel Green,
San Pietro and lots more.
978-1-910863-05-3

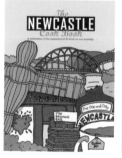

The Newcastle Cook Book
features David Coulson
of Peace & Loaf, Bealim
House, Grainger Market,
Quilliam Brothers and lots
more.
978-1-910863-04-6

The Cheshire Cook Book
features Simon Radley of
The Chester Grosvenor, The
Chef's Table, Great North
Pie Co., Harthill Cookery
School and lots more.
978-1-910863-07-7

**The Leicestershire & Rutland
Cook Book** features Tim Hart
of Hambleton Hall, John's
House, Farndon Fields,
Leicester Market, Walter
Smith and lots more.
978-0-9928981-8-2

*All books in this series are available from Waterstones,
Amazon and independent bookshops.*

FIND OUT MORE ABOUT US AT WWW.MEZEPUBLISHING.CO.UK